"ABSOLUTELY ABSORBING."
New York City Tribune

"An astonishing piece of detective work."
LIZ SMITH

"A riveting account of life in the quicksand of city politics."
New York Post

"A sobering indictment."
Publishers Weekly

"Crammed with fascinating forensic lore ... More than enough fierce fare here to please—with a vengeance—most crime buffs."
The Kirkus Reviews

"Intriguing."

Booklist

"Reads like a collection of mystery stories. Recommended."

Library Journal

UNNATURAL DEATH:

CONFESSIONS OF A MEDICAL EXAMINER

Michael M. Baden, M.D.
With
Judith Adler Hennessee

IVY BOOKS • NEW YORK

Ivy Books
Published by Ballantine Books
Copyright © 1989 by Michael M. Baden, M.D., and Judith Adler Hennessee

Library of Congress Catalog Card Number: 88-43366

ISBN 0-8041-0599-5

This edition published by arrangement with Random House, Inc.

Manufactured in the United States of America

First Ballantine Books Edition: May 1990

20 19 18 17 16 15 14 13 12 11

To Colonel Henry F. Williams,
New York State Police,
in appreciation for his legacy to the forensic sciences.

—MICHAEL M. BADEN, M.D.

To my daughter, Nancy.

—JUDITH ADLER HENNESSEE

CONTENTS

INTRODUCTION

Medical examiners are the only doctors whose patients are dead and therefore silent. They cannot explain why they died, so we have to find out in other ways. We are detectives of death—we visit the scene; we examine the medical evidence and the laboratory findings and put them together with the circumstances and the patient's medical history. Through the autopsy, we make the body speak to us. Deciphering the message is an art as well as a science.

Our medical specialty is forensic pathology. We know about the three kinds of unnatural death—suicides, homicides, and accidents. We are trained to analyze traumatic injuries—gunshot and stab wounds, blunt force, and poison. Our work is different from that of hospital pathologists who autopsy bodies to study the ravages of disease. Our methods are different from those of doctors who care for the living and whose concern is more the treatment than the cause. We want to know how the knife went in, from above or below, and where the person who wielded it was standing; which bullet hole was the entrance and which the exit and where the shot came from. Medically, these things may be irrelevant, but in a courtroom they are extremely significant in deciding the cause and manner of death and reconstructing how it happened. The kind of autopsy we do is called a medical-legal autopsy.

Forensic pathology is an untaught specialty, a stepchild of the medical profession. After medical school we get our training as apprentices in a medical examiner's office. There is even confu-

sion about our title. In some states we are called coroners, but
in most parts of the country coroners are not doctors. They tend
to be undertakers and tow-truck operators who got into the business because they could transport bodies. They hire doctors to
do autopsies. These doctors are untrained in forensic pathology
and often make mistakes. People are accused of murder and go
to trial based on those mistakes. Others escape detection, and
still others go free for lack of strong medical evidence. The
United States has no systematic, comprehensive method of certi-
fying death. There are fewer than four hundred full-time forensic pathologists in the entire country, not nearly enough to
handle the number of deaths that fall within our province. Of
the two million deaths a year in the United States, 8 percent are
unnatural. (In younger people, up to age thirty-five, the figures
are higher—more than half are unnatural.) All the obvious
homicides are autopsied; most accidents and suicides are not.
Death certificates often list the wrong cause of death.

Medical examiners (MEs) frequently see things no one else
sees, the deaths that need not have happened, the failures of society. As public doctors, our findings should be used to make public policy; instead, we are too often viewed as Cassandras, telling
people things they don't want to hear. It was an ME who first
drew attention to the problem of battered children. MEs know
that alcohol is a silent partner in almost half of all unnatural
deaths. It's an underlying cause, as in drunk driving, so it isn't
written on the death certificate. It is there in small plane crashes
and in boat accidents and accidents in the home. It is commonly
present in suicides and deaths by fire.

In the public sphere, MEs see ways to prevent death just as
other doctors see ways to prevent disease. Part of our job is to
identify new diseases, like AIDS, before they become epidemics.
We also see the results of unsafe technology, the flaws in design
that cost lives. Airplane seats were designed with metal bars attached to the bottom of the chair to hold suitcases and keep
them from sliding backwards. During crashes, people's feet were

being cut off at the ankle. One New York City ME kept a "centipede," a large tray of these feet. The danger was pointed out to the pathologist the FAA sent to observe autopsies. The bar was redesigned so that it didn't cut feet.

These techniques need not be confined to the dead. In Europe, clinical forensic pathologists are on call to hospital emergency rooms where they use the same methods of analysis with the living as with the dead. Here, with the exception of rape kits, we have been slow to take advantage of what forensic science can offer.

The case of Tawana Brawley, the black teenager who claimed to have been abducted and taken into the woods where four white men allegedly raped her for four days, might have proceded along different lines if a clinical forensic pathologist had been available at the hospital when she was brought in. Brawley, who was missing for four days in November 1987, was found in a plastic garbage bag behind the apartment building her family had been evicted from two weeks previously. Her body was smeared with feces, and "Nigger" and "KKK" were scrawled across her chest. She was brought to a hospital emergency room in Wappingers Falls, a small community in upstate New York. The situation was complicated by the fact that Brawley refused to allow the hospital to use the rape kit at first, and five hours elapsed before any evidence was taken. During that time, the attendants washed her. Even so, the photographs, the analysis of her clothing, the vaginal swabs, and the hospital and laboratory reports, which I later reviewed for the attorney general, contradicted her whole story.

If, as Brawley said, she was repeatedly raped by different men for four days, there should have been some evidence of it. There was no semen. There was not even a bruise. If the rape took place in the woods, there should have been traces of earth or pine needles or grass or leaves on her hair and clothes. There was no evidence that she had been in the woods. But there was evidence that she had been somewhere else. The FBI lab, which analyzed the feces on her clothes, found dog hairs in it. The dog hairs belonged to a pet dog that lived two apartments away from where Brawley was found. The racial slurs were also open to question. I had seen similar writings before which were self-inflicted. They had certain things in common: they were a political statement; they were written on a surface that was easily accessible to the victim, and their imprint was neither painful nor disfiguring. When these elements are present, such writing is virtually always done by the central character in the drama.

The circumstances were also strange—that Brawley would be brought to a place that had once been home and where her abductors would risk being seen and identified. There was no indication that she had been hurt or that a crime had been committed, as a grand jury would later determine, but her story was distorted and politicized by her advisors who sought to turn it into a paradigm of racial injustice. To a large extent, they succeeded. Because correct forensic procedures had not been followed immediately, there is still doubt: a great many people who don't believe Brawley's story still think *something* happened and that the system didn't work for her.

Forensic pathology is a profession with an untapped potential, one that is not properly appreciated. But it is also a profession that is enormously gratifying—it offers the adventure of detection, the excitement of discovery, the satisfaction of searching for the truth. It is a profession I have loved since I watched my first autopsy thirty-four years ago.

MICHAEL M. BADEN, M.D.
JANUARY 1989
NEW YORK CITY

1

HEROES AND
CONSPIRACIES

THE PRICE OF FAME

HEROES AND CELEBRITIES are not always granted the comfort of resting in peace. The price of fame is often a posthumous role in a conspiracy theory. When Marilyn Monroe died of an overdose of barbiturates, a small industry sprang up to prove she had been murdered. The brevity of Pope John Paul I's reign—he died suddenly after only thirty-three days in office—inspired stories of a murderous cabal that silenced him before he could put into effect threatening changes. Bobby Kennedy is said by some to have been killed by a guard who was standing near him and not by the wild shooting of Sirhan Sirhan. After J. Edgar Hoover's death, presumably of natural causes, there was talk of murder. Joan Crawford's death (she was signed out as a heart attack) drew whispers of suicide. The famous and infamous, the celebrated and notorious, do not bleed and die the way the rest of us do. They have scenarios, intricately plotted dramas. Buried villains still stalk the earth, hidden in other guises, and news of their obscure ends in faraway villages only brings disbelief. In 1979 Dr. Josef Mengele, the "Angel of

Death" at Auschwitz, drowned in Brazil, where he was living under an assumed name. He was identified unequivocally through his teeth, but many people still think he is alive. There are reports of sightings and offers of a reward for the "real" Dr. Mengele.

In this, the century of the spy, deaths are scrutinized with a view to the plotter behind the curtain, the stranger in the shadow. The hero cannot be undone by a single assailant—an oversized life demands a memorable death, one not accorded other mortals. There must be a plot to bring him down. Amelia Earhart, on the last leg of a flight around the world, disappeared in the Pacific Ocean somewhere between New Guinea and Howland Island, her next stop. It was 1937, and dark tales of espionage circulated: she was really a spy on a reconnaissance mission and the Japanese caught her and tortured her (in fact, some people think she is still a captive). What happened was more mundane. She got lost and ran out of gas. She had removed a heavy antenna from her plane. Without this device, she failed to pick up radio signals that would have directed her to Howland Island.

Even when an autopsy is done, the speculation doesn't stop. On the contrary. Marilyn Monroe's autopsy findings were used as evidence that her suicide was a murder. It was considered highly suspicious that there were no barbiturates in her stomach, which is where they are usually found after a suicidal overdose. Instead, they were only in her bloodstream. This was taken to mean that she couldn't have swallowed the pills; therefore, she must have been injected. An injection presupposed a second person. But this is jumping to conclusions. The process of absorbing liquids into the bloodstream works faster in some people than in others. Alcohol, barbiturates, and water could all have been absorbed after Monroe lost consciousness and before she died. It is possible that the toxicologists did not examine the stomach contents as carefully as they might. They were not as sophisticated then as they are now, and it's difficult to say what they might have missed.

People assume that most autopsies are done properly, that only the ones they hear about have been botched. The distinction is really between natural and unnatural death. Most natural deaths are autopsied competently or not at all. It is the autopsies of unnatural deaths that are performed ineptly, but few people know. Only those of public figures are made public.

After the assassination of Martin Luther King, Jr., the question arose whether James Earl Ray had committed the murder all by himself. Ray was carrying too much money when he was finally caught, and he was thought to be too dumb to have managed such a complex job and escaped all by himself. Dr. Jerry Francisco, the Tennessee medical examiner in Memphis (who also oversaw Elvis Presley's autopsy), waited to get permission from Coretta King to do the postmortem. When there is a murder, permission should not be required. The interests of society demand an autopsy.

Even after he was given permission, Francisco appeared overwhelmed by respect and did less than he should have. The bullet went through King's jawbone and into his neck, but Francisco didn't trace the gunshot track, which is normal procedure. Nor did he attempt to identify the black material in the wound. The material became a source of much speculation. It could have been powder grains, which would have meant that King was shot from up close, by someone standing less than a foot away. Ray was about one hundred yards away. It was like a rerun of the John F. Kennedy assassination, with the possibility that there was a second shooter and Ray was the patsy: Ray shot and missed, and someone standing next to King on the second-floor balcony of the Lorraine Motel shot him at close range.

The theory didn't work. Ten years after King's death, as part of my work on the congressional Select Committee on Assassinations (I headed the medical investigation into King's death), I sent a slide with the black stuff to McCrone Associates, a laboratory in Chicago that specializes in identifying particles. Under an ordinary microscope, with the light coming up from below, smoke, soot, carbon, and lead all look alike. They are just black spots, with no distinctive structure. The lab identified the black stuff not as gunshot powder but as lead. Lead is exactly what it should have been if it came from Ray's gun. Ray had shot King with a .30-06 soft-nosed hunting bullet. The tip of a soft-nosed bullet is lead, and when it strikes bone it breaks apart, giving it greater killing power.

In three of the "crimes of the century"—the kidnapping and murder of the Lindbergh baby, the murder of Sir Harry Oakes in 1943 in the Bahamas, and the assassination of John F. Kennedy—the autopsies, which were acceptable according to the standards of the day, were forensic disasters. The Lindbergh baby's death was attributed to a fractured skull. Years later I went over the evidence for a symposium, "Forensic Science, Then and Now," a fifty-year review of the profession given by the American Academy of Forensic Sciences. The fractured-skull diagnosis was wrong for two reasons: there was no fracture, just separation of the unfused skull bones which is normal in all babies, and there was no brain damage. It's the brain damage, not the fracture, that would cause death. The baby was probably smothered at the time of the kidnapping to keep him from crying out and alerting the family and the nurse who were all in nearby rooms.

Sir Harry Oakes, one of the richest men in the world and a confidant of the Duke and Duchess of Windsor, was discovered lying in a burning bed on his back with a bludgeoned skull. The body had been moved after death—the dried blood on his face ran up from his ears toward his nose, defying gravity. Nobody noticed. The duke, in his capacity of governor of the Bahamas, oversaw the investigation. Oakes's killer was never identified. His son-in-law was accused and tried but found not guilty.

It isn't that a well-done autopsy would have solved these murders. Conspiracies don't show up in autopsy reports, and anyway, there seems to be a need to tell stories about the lives and deaths of famous people. But an autopsy clears up the physical questions surrounding the death. We can see what happened and what didn't. It's part of the process of finding the truth.

Where bungled autopsies are concerned, President Kennedy's is the exemplar. After his death it was inevitable that conspiracy theories would arise and proliferate, but there would not have been so many errors and distortions to feed on if the autopsy had been done properly. From the beginning it was surrounded with confusion and secrecy and papered over with an enormous concern for appearances. Suspicion was created simply from the way it was managed. It opened the door to grassy knolls and second gunmen and whatever theory anyone wanted to present. It fed a conspiracy industry that mixed together the FBI, the CIA, the Mafia, the Russians, and the Cubans in a monster plot that was the culmination of our Cold War fantasies. The country could accept the myth of the Lone Ranger but not its underside, the lone assassin.

Our European counterparts in forensic medicine, more cynical and sophisticated about the uses of power than we, were skeptical of the clumsy way the Kennedy autopsy was handled. They thought it was sinister, that the clumsiness had to be officially sanctioned. At the very least, such carelessness revealed a lack of desire to find the truth. Taking it one step further, the autopsy could have been part of the conspiracy—it was deliberately sabotaged to destroy evidence.

American assassination buffs developed elaborate theories but were hampered in trying to prove them. The Kennedy family controlled access to the evidence, which was kept in the National Archives, and rarely granted anyone permission to view it, a policy that generated even more suspicion. The privately owned Zapruder film of the assassination (the main pictures available) was endlessly analyzed, sequence by sequence. Conspiracy devotees enhanced and blew up each frame; a shadow of a shadow became a face behind a tree, dark figures lurked on the fringes. They saw that Kennedy's head moved backward instead of forward after he was shot. If the bullet came from behind, they reasoned, from the Texas School Book Depository Building where the killer, Lee Harvey Oswald, was shooting from, then the impact would have forced the head forward. Since the head moved backward, they said, JFK was shot from the front, which meant there were two shooters, one from the grassy knoll. This theory is not unreasonable; it's just wrong. They left out of their calculations the acceleration of the car Kennedy was riding in. Beyond that, the body simply does not react that way. The force of the bullet would just as likely cause Kennedy's head to move forward as backward. It's not predictable.

In 1977 Congress set up the Select Committee on Assassinations to resolve these and other vexing questions. I was asked to take charge of the forensic pathology investigation, and I assembled a panel of eight other medical examiners. I thought nine of us would have more credibility than one. Among us, we had performed over 100,000 medical-legal autopsies. (Other panels investigated nonforensic areas—the Cubans, the Mafia, the photographs, etc.)

Even at the very beginning in 1963, there were rumblings within the community of medical examiners that the autopsy was a disaster, and that Commander James J. Humes, who had done it, was not trained for it. In fact, he had never autopsied anyone with a gunshot wound. The leading critic of the autopsy was Dr. Cyril Wecht (who later served on my committee), the coroner/ME of Pittsburgh. Wecht was forthright, outspoken, and saw no virtue in being diplomatic in this matter. It was a secret autopsy done by a man who was not competent for the job, he said, but he didn't get any points for saying out loud what his peers knew. His complaint looked like sour grapes, and many forensic pathologists, even though they agreed with him, thought him irresponsible and self-serving for making it. In contrast, Milton Helpern, the highly respected chief medical examiner of New York City and the soul of diplomacy, suggested in an interview that the government should have called in competent MEs to assist Humes. Some of the leading MEs in the country were in Baltimore, Philadelphia, and New York. In fact, Earl Rose, the Dallas coroner, was a trained forensic pathologist. As a result of the interview, Helpern thought, his name was removed from a list of lecturers to the Armed Forces Institute of Pathology (a federal training program for pathologists).

After the assassination, Kennedy was brought to Parkland Hospital where he was pronounced dead. There are television clips of Earl Rose, standing at the door of the hospital like Horatius at the bridge, saying no to the Secret Service men, no, they couldn't remove the body, and the Secret Service men telling him to get out of the way or he would be run over. They almost had a fistfight.

The Dallas coroner had jurisdiction over the body. Murder was a state crime. Legally, Kennedy should not have been moved, but in this situation other considerations overrode the legal ones. At that early stage, no one knew who had shot the President or if Lyndon Johnson was also in danger. The Secret Service wanted LBJ out of Dallas and back in Washington. Mrs. Kennedy also wanted the body out and refused to leave without it. In the end, the Kennedy entourage physically pushed Rose out of the way and rushed to the airport. They were worried that the Dallas police might chase them. They knew they were taking the body illegally.

No forensic pathologist has ever examined the body of the President. We did our investigation by reviewing the medical and autopsy reports, the photographs and X rays and clothing. It had not occurred to the Warren Commission (which was set up shortly after the assassination to investigate it) that a forensic pathologist could contribute anything to the proceedings. Among its illustrious members—Chief Justice Earl Warren, former CIA director Allen W. Dulles, Representative Gerald R. Ford, and others—there was no one who had any appreciation of forensic medicine and the mysteries it could clarify. They were unaware that there were two kinds of autopsies, the usual hospital one and the forensic one, or that it mattered that Commander Humes didn't know the difference between an entrance wound and an exit wound. They didn't know the difference, either. They thought a pathologist was a pathologist, and one could do as good an autopsy as another. And so, many of the questions that the Warren Commission thought it had answered in 1964 were still unresolved in 1977. Our job was to answer them: to pinpoint where the bullets had entered and exited, and to trace their trajectories. Did they come from behind, where Oswald was, or from the grassy knoll in front? From above, or from ground level? Could a single bullet have gone through both Kennedy and Governor John Connally and emerged "pristine"? How many shots were fired? Was Oswald the only shooter?

In doing the investigation, we literally had to begin at the beginning. The variety of conspiracy theories had called into question every bit of evidence, including the body itself. According to one scenario, during the plane ride from Dallas to Washington the entrance wounds were altered to look like exit wounds in order to confuse everyone about the direction of the shots. According to another, the original autopsy report, photographs, and X rays had all been stolen from the National Archives and replaced with fakes. I wondered at the vast numbers of people that would have been required to carry out all these tasks and the extraordinary combination of luck, competence, and intelligence, so lacking in all other human endeavors, that would have been needed to pull off these delicate and complex conspiracies in secret—and have them remain secret.

Our first order of business was to determine whether the photographs and X rays were indeed those of President Kennedy. A number of doctors had treated JFK, and they supplied us with his old skull X rays. They matched those in the archive. Lowell Levine, our forensic dentist, identified them from the teeth. The family balked at having X rays of the head published in our final report. That distinctive Kennedy jaw was the source of some anguish—it looked too much like him, they said. We compromised. In the published report, the lower part of the jaw, showing the teeth, is blocked out. To my knowledge, this was the only thing the family censored. The report itself was published as written.

As the archive gave up its secrets, we realized that everything wasn't there. Kennedy's brain, which had been removed during the autopsy and placed in the archive, was missing, and so were the microscopic slides of tissues, and the paraffin blocks in which tissue is hardened. They had simply disappeared. We didn't think anyone had made a deliberate effort to mislead us or destroy evidence—the most important things, all the photographs and X rays, were there. We thought perhaps the missing material had been buried with the President at Arlington, but an exhumation was out of the question. The family had not been enthusiastic about this investigation. It was just a painful reminder. The location of the missing items is still a mystery, but their disappearance is not particularly sinister. Memorabilia of the famous have a way of vanishing into doctors' private collections. That is what happened to Einstein's brain. In the 1950s, Martin Luther King was treated at Harlem Hospital for a stab wound in the chest. In 1978, when we tried to get his medical records and X rays for the committee, they were missing. The administrator had put them in a safe, but somehow they had disappeared.

Kennedy's body was brought to Bethesda Naval Hospital at about 7:35 P.M. on November 22. Commander Humes, the chief pathologist, was not sanguine about doing the autopsy. He knew he had never done one like it before. Why not request help? I asked him. He explained that he couldn't—he was low man in the hierarchy, and he had to follow orders; in the military, you don't tell generals and admirals that you are unqualified for the job. And he had been reassured that Colonel Pierre Finck, the head of wounds ballistics at the Armed Forces Institute of Pathology, was coming to assist and observe. Finck, he figured, knew about bullet holes.

Colonel Finck, it turned out, had never done an autopsy involving a gunshot wound, either. For almost a decade he had been in charge of reviewing the records of U.S. military personnel who had died of gunshot wounds. Two people who were not professionally trained in what they were doing were watching each other. Finck didn't offer guidance because it never occurred to him that Humes needed any. When Finck didn't speak, Humes thought he was doing the job right.

Humes was also getting other signals. He understood, he told us, that he wasn't really supposed to do a full autopsy. He was just supposed to find the bullet. (Everyone thought the bullet that had hit the President in the back was still in his body.) This idea was conveyed so obliquely that Humes couldn't explain exactly how he knew. Somehow, he absorbed it from the FBI and the Secret Service. They hadn't given him any orders. Talking to him was like talking to the people who did the Vietnam body counts—they didn't have to be told what was wanted. It wasn't necessary to spell out anything for Humes. It was apparent that the body had been brought to Bethesda against the coroner's objections, to accommodate the wishes of the family. Humes understood, he told us, that the Kennedys were not interested in having an autopsy done. He also knew that religious Catholics tend to be opposed to autopsies. And he was not in a position to press the issue.

The room was chaotic. Generals, admirals, and cabinet members milled around, shocked. Humes, a mere commander, seemingly had no control of his own autopsy room. He was there to please his superiors. He felt it was beyond his powers to describe the wounds and decided to rely on photographs. "The complexity of these fractures and the fragments thus produced," he wrote in the autopsy report, "tax satisfactory verbal description and are better appreciated in photographs and roentgenograms which are prepared." The photographer was there, the corpsman who usually took pictures of damaged hearts and cirrhotic livers and other diseases. He was snapping away when he caught the attention of an FBI agent, who came up to him and asked for his clearance. "Clearance?" said the corpsman. "This is my job." The agent took away his camera, exposed all the film, and threw him out. (The exposed film is in the archive.) "We've got our own man taking pictures," the FBI agent said. The FBI photographer, who had clearance, was in the same quandary as Humes. He had never taken autopsy pictures before and was untrained in photographing gunshot wounds. His pictures showed it. A proper photograph would have shown the injury first as it was and then cleaned off, next to a ruler to give perspective on its size and position in the body. None of his pictures clearly defined the entrance or exit wounds. The photographs of the body's interior were out of focus. You have to know at what level you want to shoot—the chest is deep. He didn't take pictures of any internal organs. These are the pictures Humes proposed to rely on, his own descriptive powers having failed him.

Given all these ambiguities and conflicting purposes, the autopsy itself was woefully inadequate. Before the President was buried, no one, either in Dallas or in Washington, looked at both sides of the body, front and back, and realized that a bullet had entered the back and exited the throat. The people in Dallas never turned Kennedy over and never saw the back wound. Humes didn't figure things out until after the President was lying in state in the Rotunda.

The President arrived at Bethesda with a massive head wound, a back wound, and a throat wound. Humes, who was stymied, did not call Dallas to find out which hospital medical procedures had been performed that had bruised or altered the body before it arrived at Bethesda. Therefore, he did not know that a tracheostomy had been performed through the exit wound in the throat. Dallas thought the President had been shot in the throat and was trying to help him breathe. Humes saw the entrance wound in the back, but he didn't connect it with the throat wound, where the bullet had exited. (As it happened, this was the so-called "pristine" bullet that went on to wound John Connally, but no one knew that until later.)

Humes took X rays to see if the bullet was still inside the body. Nothing showed up on the X rays, and he told the FBI the bullet had entered the back, gone in a few inches, and then fallen out of the same hole it entered. But bullets don't do that. As a bullet passes through the body, the track it makes collapses on itself. The bullet can't back out. He couldn't understand what had happened to the head bullet, either. (The Connally bullet was found on a stretcher in the hospital. The Kennedy head bullet was found on the floor of Kennedy's car in front. It had struck the windshield strut and broken in two.)

It took Humes about two hours to do the autopsy. He spent the rest of the night (from midnight to 5:30 A.M.) helping the mortician embalm the body and put the skull together. The autopsy should reasonably have taken the better part of a day. A complicated one can take eight hours, and this one was complicated. The autopsy is not finished until you work out the bullet tracks along with the exits and entrances. Humes explained that he was in a hurry, that the family was waiting for the body.

Humes took notes of his autopsy findings, but he didn't stay to write the report. He'd been in the morgue since 7:30 the previous night (Friday, November 22), and at 5:30 A.M. he was exhausted. He also had to take his daughter to her confirmation on Saturday morning.

When he returned on Saturday afternoon, he noticed there was a problem with his notes. They were stained with blood. Humes was a fastidious man; he cared about appearances, and the blood disturbed him. He remembered having visited Abraham Lincoln's birthplace in Illinois and seeing an antimacassar that had been taken from Ford's Theatre. It had bloodstains on it, and Humes thought how unseemly it was for Lincoln's blood to be on public view. He was deeply concerned about the Kennedy family's feelings and told the committee, "The original notes which were stained with the blood of our late President, I felt, were inappropriate to retain to turn in to anyone in that condition. I felt that people with some peculiar ideas about the value of that type of material, they might fall into their hands." There was only one thing to do, and he did it. He burned his notes. The missing notes added to the paranoia, the belief that there had to be a conspiracy.

That afternoon Humes did what should have been done when the body arrived at Bethesda—he called Dallas. He spoke to Dr. Malcolm Perry, one of the doctors who had attended Kennedy in Parkland Hospital, and learned about the tracheostomy through the bullet hole in the throat. The light dawned. He hadn't known there was a bullet hole in the throat at all. He'd thought it was just a tracheostomy. He now realized that the tracheostomy incorporated the exit wound, and he understood that he hadn't been able to find the bullet because it had gone into Kennedy's back and out his throat. But by then it was too late to trace the bullet track, so Humes tried to figure it out from memory. The Warren Commission drawing shows it starting high on the back and moving downward and out the throat. It is wrong. The X rays and photographs show the wound to be lower on the back and the track slightly upward. Fifteen years later at our interview, Humes excused himself by saying he didn't have any photographs of the autopsy to refer to.

Humes worked on the autopsy report from Saturday afternoon until about 3:00 P.M. Sunday, doing the best he could under difficult circumstances. It is not clear what facts he used from his original notes. Since he wrote the final report after talking to Dallas, he incorporated some material that he didn't see with his own eyes. The result was an autopsy report filled with errors, sins of omission and commission. Bullets weren't tracked, the brain wasn't sectioned, the measurements were inaccurate, the head wound wasn't described. The weights and measures of body organs made no sense. The liver was down as weighing 650 grams—one and a half pounds—which is too light to sustain life. An adult liver weighs a little over three pounds. Other organs—the pancreas, the prostate—were not described at all. The collarbones weren't separated from the breastbone to permit an examination of the neck organs. The entire neck area was undisturbed by the autopsy, which is one reason why Humes couldn't trace that bullet track. He didn't shave any hair from around the head wounds in order to examine them. The wounds were photographed through the hair.

One of the things that had haunted the President was his Addison's disease. Over the years, rumors that he was debilitated by it had surfaced and been denied. It was a well-kept secret, and the family wanted it to remain one. In the early 1960s, public officials had an easier time keeping secrets. The concept that the press had the right to know every intimate detail of a President's life was not yet in vogue. Civilians, such as the medical people at Parkland Hospital, couldn't be controlled, but the military could be trusted.

Addison's disease is an atrophying of the adrenal cortex, the glands that make cortisone, a hormone that regulates the electrolyte balance of sodium and potassium. An imbalance causes progressive weakness, weight loss, and death. At one time the disease was fatal; now you take cortisone to replace what your body cannot manufacture. Cortisone causes odd fat deposits— an upper-back hump, full cheeks. Kennedy had them both, but Addison's disease is not mentioned in the autopsy report, nor are the adrenal glands. It is standard procedure to describe them. I asked Commander Humes about it when he came to Washington to testify before the committee. Even then, fifteen years later, when it no longer mattered, his feelings of respect were so strong that he refused to comment for the record about Addison's disease. The family didn't want any mention of any diseases that might be present, he said. However, several doctors had treated Kennedy for Addison's and taken X rays of his pituitary gland, the gland at the base of the skull that controls the adrenals. He had had a number of sets of X rays taken. The doctors had also written reports. The adrenals were very tiny—the disease had atrophied them.

Perhaps the most egregious error was the four-inch miscalculation. The head is only five inches long from crown to neck, but Humes was confused by a little piece of brain tissue that had adhered to the scalp. He placed the head wound four inches lower than it actually was, near the neck instead of the cowlick.

Despite all these errors and for the wrong reasons, Humes came to the right conclusions—that Kennedy had been shot by two bullets from behind, one in the head and one in the back. They were in the wrong place and badly tracked, but he got the two most important things right.

In reconstructing the events, we were hindered by not having all the evidence we needed to work with. We had X rays of some things, pictures of others, X rays and descriptions of still others. We also had Kennedy's clothes. The shirt and jacket each had a round bullet hole in the back. The pictures of the President were unfocused, but helpful. They showed the burn of an "abrasion collar," a redness on the skin surrounding the entrance wound, in the same place where the clothes were torn. That was the entrance wound. In front, the throat wound had been distorted by the tracheostomy (an ordinary exit wound pushes the skin out), but the clothes again saved the day. There were slitlike tears on the tie and shirt collar that were typical of an exit wound. Exits look like little cuts.

For the head wound, we enhanced the X rays and saw the entrance perforation on top of the cowlick. Pictures of the wound yielded more when viewed through a stereopticon. In three dimensions they showed the oblique lines (beveling) on the bone in the back of the skull that an entering bullet makes. Only the top part—the cerebrum—was injured by the bullet track, which couldn't have happened if the bullet had been four inches lower. We also used a little common sense. Humes had placed the wound four inches below where it was, but the cowlick was right in the center of the FBI photograph. A photographer tries to center his picture.

We reconstructed the exit wound at the throat from X rays of the skull and skull fragments and photographs of a single piece of bone which came to be called the Nieman-Marcus fragment. Three skull fragments had been retrieved from the limousine, brought to Washington, X-rayed, and later vanished. The fourth, measuring about two by one and a half inches, was found a few days after the autopsy by a premed student walking his dog in Dealey Plaza, where the shots were fired. He took it home to his father, a doctor, who knew what it was and had it photographed. At a party, the photographer couldn't resist talking about it, and the story got back to the FBI. Agents swooped down on the premed student, who was saving the fragment as a souvenir. He had it wrapped in a piece of cotton in a Nieman-Marcus box. It later disappeared from the archive, along with the other fragments, but the photographs of it were good enough for purposes of reconstructing the skull.

There was no evidence that anything had hit the President from the front.

Near the end of the hearings, John Connally came to Washington to testify. One of the last and most baffling problems was the mystery surrounding the magic bullet, the bullet that went through two people—into Kennedy's back and out of his throat; into Connally's back (he was sitting in the jump seat with his back to Kennedy) just above his right armpit, injuring his lung and fifth rib, and exiting in front below his right nipple, then into his right wrist near the thumb, through the radius bone above the wrist and out of the undersurface of the wrist, and finally part way into his left thigh and out. It was a very acrobatic bullet. Connally was convinced that it never happened, that he was shot with a separate bullet entirely.

The bullet was an Italian 6.5 millimeter, for a Mannlicher–Carcano rifle—a military, not a civilian, bullet. In conformity with the Geneva Convention rules of civilized warfare, military ammunition is made with a full metal jacket. The idea is that the bullet will not break up inside the body but go through it, causing less pain and suffering. Police ammunition is usually not jacketed. It is soft enough so that when it hits a body the nose of the bullet flattens, slowing it down. It doesn't go through the body and hit someone else. An unjacketed bullet could not have performed the way this metal-jacketed one did. It was able to accomplish so much because it went through soft tissue. In its passage through Kennedy, it did not strike bone. Once inside Connally, it struck a very thin bone—a rib—which did not slow it down significantly. The only bone of substance it struck was Connally's right wristbone, after which it was almost spent and barely managed to penetrate Connally's left thigh. It was found on a stretcher at Parkland Hospital.

Believers in the existence of a second shooter on the grassy knoll called it the pristine bullet, indestructible, but it was damaged; it is flat on one side. The FBI ballistics examination concluded that the bullet matched Oswald's rifle, but this did not satisfy the conspiracy buffs. They scoffed at such a simplistic connection. Of course it matched, they said; it was planted on the stretcher to mislead everyone into thinking Oswald was the lone assassin. It had the right markings for Oswald's weapon, but it really came from the firing range where he had honed his marksmanship; it had not been fired in Dealey Plaza. We had to resolve that question.

First, had the bullet burrowed into Connally's thigh bone? If it had, it couldn't have leaped out and fallen onto the stretcher. In one of the X rays of Connally's leg, there is a tiny sliver of metal adjacent to the femur. Everyone concluded the obvious— that the bullet had come in and hit the bone. But a bullet that goes two inches deep and into bone doesn't suddenly decide to reverse itself. (Humes made the same mistake with JFK. He thought the bullet in the back had retraced its steps and fallen out. It was this same bullet.) It can't just drop out of the same hole unless it is very close to the surface. From one of Connally's

X rays, it looked as if the bullet was next to or in the thighbone. But the X ray was a lateral one, a side view, and you can't see depth on it. In the archive is another X ray, a front view that shows the sliver is clearly not in bone. It's just under the skin. It did not hit the femur. The bullet, its energy gone by then, only penetrated the first layers of skin. Only half an inch of it went in. The penetration was shallow enough for it to have fallen out and landed on the stretcher.

Next, was the Connally bullet the same one that had been found on the stretcher? A tiny fragment of bullet was removed from Connally's wrist in Parkland Hospital and put into the archive. We took it, together with the bullet from the stretcher, and sent it to a special laboratory in California. The lab does neutron activation analysis, a technique for finding trace amounts of heavy metals that is so sensitive it can distinguish between two bullets on an assembly line. The trace metal content in the bullet found on the stretcher and the fragment from Connally's wrist matched perfectly. It was a copper-jacketed military bullet with a core of 99 percent lead and insignificant amounts of strontium, arsenic, nickel, platinum, and silver. As small as they are, these traces are like fingerprints.

There was one last thing about this bullet that I could only resolve by firsthand observation. According to Connally's medical records, the bullet struck him nose first in the back and left a vertical scar. I thought the records were wrong. If it was the same magic bullet, it would have gone in sideways—with the length, not the point, first. After leaving Kennedy, it would have lost its power and become a tumbling bullet, and tumbling bullets rotate. When they finally strike, they strike edgewise. I needed to examine Connally.

In 1978, John Connally was running for the presidency. He came to Washington to testify before the committee and agreed to let me examine his scars in his suite at the Mayflower Hotel. He was an impressive-looking man with a presidential air, a man who behaved as if he had important things to do. His manner was affable and confident. Connally wasn't too happy with the whole enterprise. I was a stranger; why should I be allowed to examine him? He had given permission, yes, but it was awkward. Amenities, formalities, had to be gone through. His wife, Nellie, was there, and an aide, Julian Reed. I mentioned the name of a good friend in Corpus Christi, an offshore-oil man, who was also a friend of Reed's and a contributor to the campaign. The social connection made things less uncomfortable when I asked Connally to take off his clothes.

He removed his shirt. There it was—a two-inch-long sideways entrance scar in his back. He had not been shot by a second shooter but by the same flattened bullet that went through Kennedy. I wanted to see the thigh wound, but I had to let it go. I could not bring myself to ask him to take off his pants. The Corpus Christi friendship was not close enough for that, and Connally was in a hurry—he had a plane to catch.

Connally remained unconvinced. He had been in Dallas, and he knew. He said he heard a shot, turned partly around, and then he was shot. This could well have happened if the first shot missed both him and Kennedy (Oswald fired three times), but Connally thinks the first shot hit the President and the second hit him.

The following day, I testified that there had been one shooter, Oswald; three shots from behind Kennedy; and two wounds. There was no entrance wound in front. The President had been killed by a lone assassin. Forensically, we had proved it beyond a doubt.

G. Robert Blakey, the chief counsel of the Committee on Assassinations, tended to agree with Connally—he didn't think a single bullet could do that much damage. All along he had questioned and poked at every point of proof as we brought it in, as he should. I thought he was only playing devil's advocate at first, but he had a theory of his own and he wanted support for it.

Blakey came from a background of investigating organized

crime, and came to believe there was a conspiracy. He had been immersed in the Mafia for years. He had written books about it—*Racket Bureaus,* and three volumes of *Perspectives on the Investigation of Organized Crime.* The Mafia was his life's work, and the committee became important in furthering that work. In 1981, two years after the hearings, he published *The Plot to Kill the President.* (His coauthor, Richard N. Billings, the editorial director of the committee, was chronicling our progress in 1979.) Blakey believed there were two shooters, Oswald in the book building and an unknown on the grassy knoll. If there were two shooters, the assassination had to be defined as a conspiracy, and he had a theory that linked it to the Mafia. Blakey's only hard scientific evidence came from a Dallas police department tape which belonged to a motorcycle cop. The cop had inadvertently left his radio on transmission at the time of the shooting. The tape at police headquarters had been saved because it had another homicide report on it. Early on, I had listened to it and found it indecipherable. To my ears it was valueless. All of a sudden, when the investigation was almost over and it was clear we weren't coming up with any forensic evidence that suggested a conspiracy, Blakey resurrected it. He wanted a second review of the acoustical evidence.

First, he brought in a group of acoustics experts who were famous in Washington for having worked with the Nixon tapes. They couldn't make anything out of this one. Then he called in a pair of acoustics professors from Queens College in New York. They interpreted the static on the radio and announced they heard three definite gunshot sounds and a 70 percent definite fourth. The probable fourth shot came one second after the third. The total amount of time for the four shots was eight seconds. It was physically impossible for Oswald, with the rifle he used, to have fired four shots within that time, which meant there was a second shooter—and a conspiracy.

The science of acoustics had even more to reveal. From the sound vectors—the pattern of the sound waves—the experts said they could tell the direction of the bullets, and the sound vectors were going straight to Kennedy's head from the grassy knoll. I listened to the tape, too, but all I could hear was static. Or possibly backfire.

Blakey was very impressed. The hearings were being broadcast live on public television. Each night, the committee staff prepared for the next day's testimony. I would sit down and explain my opinions, and the staff would try to knock holes in them. It was like an informal doctoral examination. There were no surprises, but there was no script, either. I had already testified, but Blakey scheduled me to go on again, following the acoustics professors. He asked me if I could say that my forensic evidence was consistent with the acoustical findings. "Consistent with" is one of those catch-all phrases that means something could be possible. It is used a lot in our profession, especially on the witness stand when evidence can be interpreted in more than one way. All Blakey wanted me to say was that a grassy-knoll bullet might have struck the President. I didn't believe that. Forensically speaking, I was certain that absolutely nothing from that grassy knoll had hit the President.

On the final day of the hearings, just before I was due to testify, Blakey decided we were running out of time and scratched me. I have always thought that there would have been enough time for me if I had been more in tune with the acoustics experts.

The acoustics theory won the day and became the basic scientific evidence for a conspiracy. The committee decided that 70 percent was a high enough margin to suspend disbelief in a fourth shot. The members' willingness to do so indicates that they had other compelling reasons—nonmedical ones—and without the acoustical evidence they wouldn't have been able to support the conspiracy idea. The members were not particularly knowledgeable about the forensic evidence. Before I testified, I was asked by an aide to distribute a series of questions to them so they would know what to ask me to look good on camera.

The committee ended its deliberations with a hybrid theory. It concluded that three shots were fired from behind by Oswald, that two of them hit Kennedy and one missed him; and that a fourth bullet was fired by an unknown assailant from the grassy knoll and also missed him. The committee voted to pass its findings along to the FBI with a mandate to search for the second shooter. The FBI listened to the tape too, but couldn't get past the static. It rejected the mandate.

The verdict on the assassination is unchanged. On the twenty-fifth anniversary of Kennedy's death, the same old conspiracy theories were dragged out, dusted off, and presented to the public all over again, as if our investigation had resolved nothing. People went on thinking what they wanted to think.

2

THE EDUCATION OF A MEDICAL EXAMINER

LIFE AND DEATH, UPTOWN AND DOWNTOWN

MY CAREER BEGAN almost without my realizing it, and years went by before I became aware that I had chosen it. I had never heard of forensic medicine before going to medical school. I planned to be an internist and follow in the footsteps of my Nobel Prize–winning mentors, Dickinson Richards and Andre Cournand at Bellevue Hospital. But doctors, like everyone else, go where their personalities and emotional needs lead them. The confident, aggressive ones usually go into surgery. A disproportionate number of future psychiatrists have emotional problems in medical school. Pathologists and researchers prefer academic medicine—they would rather relate to microscopes and other doctors than talk to patients. Forensic pathologists are comfortable in the limelight and enjoy talking to the public. We have to be articulate. We bear witness. Our tradition is to give testimony in court. There's an early, unwitting job description of a forensic doctor in the account of the death of Julius Caesar by Suetonius, the gossip. After Caesar was stabbed, says Suetonius, he was examined by a physician named Antistius. Antistius then went to the Forum and told the assembled Senators that Caesar had twenty-three stab wounds, one of which was fatal.

I liked the public side of it. The excitement and the immediacy of it appealed to me. Every morning on the radio there were stories of murders, of plane crashes, of violence in the night, and I would go to work and see the results in front of me. More than anything I liked the instant gratification that came from doing an autopsy and knowing the diagnosis right away. Once, while I was still a student, we zoomed up the East Side Highway to Harlem in a police car. The cop drove on the wrong side—he headed north on the south drive. It was the most amazing thing, as if the Red Sea were parting in front of us.

I liked the reporters and the television cameras. The fact that they were covering my work added importance to it, an extra dimension. The visibility counterbalanced the low esteem in which we were held by the rest of the medical profession. Forensic pathology was filled with misfits. It was considered a dumping ground for incompetents, a field that alcoholics descended into, a refuge for doctors who couldn't make it in the real world.

Anatomy fascinated me. As a medical student I was drawn to the morgue at Bellevue because the bodies were there. The autopsy room was a huge cavernous space with long windows and a twenty-foot ceiling. It was not air-conditioned. The elements of pathology that excited me were all there in my first visit—the mystery, the thrill of discovery, the rigor of research, the connection with public health, the talk with respected medical advisers. When I came in, a group of doctors was standing on one side of this enormous room while Milton Helpern, the chief medical examiner, stood on the other, doing an autopsy all by himself. The body was a thirty-five-year-old man who had died of what everyone feared was smallpox. The other doctors wouldn't go near the body. It was a matter of caution. We had all been immunized. I walked over to look. The case was unique even then. This was 1955, and the last smallpox illness in the city had been in 1947. It was essential to diagnose it quickly.

It was clear how important the ME's office was, what a profound effect it could have on public health. If the disease was smallpox, the whole city might have to be immunized.

Helpern permitted me to assist him, and when it was over he sent me to the library to research old articles in dusty journals from the 1880s that compared smallpox to similar diseases and explained how to tell them apart. Certain forms of chicken pox, I learned, could look like smallpox. I talked to the chairman of the pediatrics department, who had done work on fatal chicken pox in children.

When the microscopic tissue studies that Helpern had prepared came back, we found out that the man had an underlying lymphoma and was getting cortisone treatments for it. His immune system had been knocked out by the lymphoma, and the massive doses of cortisone made him more susceptible to other infections. (Cortisone in smaller doses does not have this effect.) The man had hemorrhagic chicken pox. Because of his immunosuppressed state, he died of it, just as AIDS kills today.

Helpern adopted me and became my mentor. After a major plane crash he took the time to explain things to me and encouraged me to do autopsies with the professionals. He liked the old European concept of the professor with a retinue of students learning from him and beholden to him. For years no medical student had cared about the medical examiner's office, and suddenly there I was, caring. He was short of people—not many go into this field—and he needed all the help he could get, but that didn't matter; I was very taken with the whole thing, and with the way he was taken with me.

All during my years in medical school and as a resident, I moonlighted in the ME's office. I saw that the process of death investigation mirrored society, that money and power played the same role in death as in life. Helpern sent me on all kinds of cases. One night he sent me to the Plaza Hotel to sign a death certificate. There, at a black-tie fund-raising dinner to benefit

Presbyterian Hospital, in a ballroom full of prominent doctors, two of whom were flanking her at the table, a woman had died.

A tablemate had asked Helpern to smooth the way for removal of the body. The doctors thought it was a heart attack. Two of them were sitting with the body in a back room (it would have been unseemly to abandon it to a waiter), and they wanted it taken to a funeral parlor as soon as possible so they could get back to their table. According to the law, the body could not be removed without a death certificate, and none of the doctors there could issue one. If the woman had died of a disease, the doctor who had treated her for it could have issued a certificate, but she hadn't even been under treatment. The death had been sudden, and only someone from the ME's office could sign the certificate.

The dinner was still in progress when I arrived. The woman, who had been a big contributor, lay on a makeshift table. She wore a long, glittering silver lamé dress. I thought there was a possibility that she had choked on a bolus of food (the French call such a death a "café coronary"; it looks like a heart attack but it's really food), but her tablemates disagreed. The two things that people have the most trouble swallowing are steak and shrimp. People with bad teeth try to get around the difficulty of chewing them by swallowing bites whole. One of the doctors said no, definitely not; she had started with her vegetable and potato; and she hadn't even gotten to her meat yet, and besides, she had a history of heart disease. What had happened was very clear to them. They didn't need to know any more than they already knew. She had been eating and talking, and all of a sudden she couldn't talk, and then she slumped forward and fell into her food. The other doctor, a retired professor of surgery, had stuck his finger into her mouth and examined her throat and found no obstruction. I told them I wouldn't do a full autopsy, but I had to examine her neck to make certain she hadn't choked on her food. They were upset, but they agreed.

They had no choice. The funeral director was waiting to take her out.

I had no equipment with me. I had called the office on the way home. The maître d' got a small kitchen knife, and I made an incision near the Adam's apple. A big bright green broccoli florette was lodged in the airway, blocking it. In his effort to help, the surgeon had just pushed it in farther. He had been drinking, I noticed, and hadn't been careful enough. Nobody congratulated me on my diagnosis. "When can we get the body released to the funeral director?" they wanted to know.

When I finished, I drove to the South Bronx. A call had come earlier to go there, but Helpern had wanted me to take care of the body at the Plaza first. The dinner guests were important people, and he didn't want them to be inconvenienced. In the Bronx there was a dead baby. A single cop sat in the hallway, reading a book, waiting for me. No car was parked on the street to show the way. The inequalities of life continue into death. On Park or Fifth Avenue, the police send three or four cars. You always know exactly where to go. In the South Bronx, a single car drops the cop off. He calls in when the doctor is finished and is picked up.

The cop let me into the apartment as if he owned it, as if the people who lived there didn't exist. They hardly noticed. They were a lively family—even though it was close to midnight, the mother and her four small children were up and running around. There were no tears. The room was small and musty. Wiring hung from the ceiling, patched together; the electricity was stolen from the apartment next door. The dead baby lay in an old crib. There was a pink Princess telephone—Welfare paid for it—and across the room in a corner, the perfect skeleton of a small rat. An odor of decaying food rose from the sink, littered with half-eaten TV dinners. I couldn't find anything wrong with the baby. The ME's office sent the morgue wagon for the body. At the autopsy the next day, the lungs were heavy and filled with

fluid, bacteria, and white blood cells. The baby had died of un-
treated pneumonia.

On another nocturnal excursion, I visited a man in his seventies whose Lower West Side apartment was on the top floor of
a four-story walkup. It was a natural death. Most of the deaths
we investigate are natural. There just isn't any other doctor
around to sign the death certificate. At first I thought he might
have been murdered. The apartment looked as if it had been ran-
sacked. Drawers were open; clothes were strewn across the
floor. The police had done it, looking for identification. The man
was lying in bed wearing a white polo shirt, black pants, and
slippers and socks. Under his shirt was a peculiar-looking belt
with zippers on the underside. I said to the cop on guard, "Hey,
he's got a money belt." I had never seen anyone wearing one
before. The cop was surprised. "Gee whiz, Doc, I missed it,"
he said. I unzipped it and found $40. "List it in the inventory,"
I told him. He was grateful. Cops get demerits for overlooking
things at the scene.

Later, in the office, when I was telling the MEs the story, they
laughed at my naïveté. By not questioning the amount, I may
have legitimized a theft. Who carries only $40 in a money belt?
When someone dies alone, it's open season on his possessions.
People tramp in and out of the apartment—the Emergency
Medical Service, the cops, the mortuary personnel, the ME. The
cops search for a medical history, the name of the doctor, the
names of the next of kin, and during the extensive rummaging,
things of value—cash, jewelry, stamp collections—disappear.
It's rare that the relatives even know that anything is missing
or, knowing, can prove it. Traps have been set and people have
been caught, but it still goes on.

I was surprised at how little sorrow there is for the dead. So
many of our clients are drug addicts or alcoholics, and the families have already used up their grief, or written the person off.
A twenty-four-year-old woman was brought in, a heroin overdose with needle scars and fresh puncture marks. They repre-

sented years of family disruptions, of tears and rage and despair. Her father, a professor, came down to identify her. He sat in the lobby in his dark blue suit reading the *Wall Street Journal,* totally uninvolved, oblivious to everything around him. When I spoke to him, he assumed the attitude of a man who had come for a job interview. He looked at his daughter and said yes, that's my daughter—is there anything else? She had died for him a long time ago. He signed the paper and left.

I also remember a woman in her twenties with a husband in his seventies who had died suddenly. They lived in an expensive apartment with very little in it except a collection of pornographic books. They had been married less than a year. The wife was distraught, in tears. The police had already interviewed her and the neighbors when I arrived. She told them he had died in his sleep of a heart attack. They were satisfied. I didn't see any injuries to the body or evidence of pills or drugs. Everything seemed in order. The funeral director was on his way over. She wanted the body cremated.

The next evening I saw her again in a French restaurant. She was the center of attraction at a party, joyful and radiant. The other tables were sedate; hers was lively. The noise caught my attention. She was in the middle of a laugh when she saw me; she stifled it and nodded. Then she whispered to a friend and the table quieted down. I felt a twinge, but the husband had already been cremated.

My first homicide had little to do with forensic medicine. It was a crime-and-punishment case, a tale of vengeance and power. In 1963 I was still a resident at Bellevue trying to make up my mind about my medical career and still moonlighting nights and weekends at the ME's office. They let me do everything except murders. Murders were too important for a novice. But this time, when the call came at 2:00 A.M., the ME in charge didn't feel like getting out of bed, and he asked me to go in his place. I was on duty anyway. It was a big vote of confidence.

The case was a shootout at the old New Yorker Hotel, at 34th

Street and Eighth Avenue. Police cars surrounded the entrance, their lights flashing. Television cameras were there, and reporters interviewed me. There had been a huge manhunt for this killer. Upstairs, Frank Falco, the dead man, lay on the bed in his shorts, his head and chest riddled with bullet holes. The Trantino case, as it came to be known, became a *cause célèbre* and is still reverberating.

On a hot August night, Falco and his partner, Thomas Trantino, had held up a bar in Lodi, New Jersey. Two cops responded to a call for help but were overpowered. Falco and Trantino were sadistic and looking for thrills. They ordered the cops to strip and perform fellatio on them, and at the moment of orgasm they shot the cops in the head. Afterward, they danced. The police force never forgot and never forgave.

They found Falco a week later. They surrounded his room; one came in through the door and another through the window from the fire escape. They told me they were on the verge of arresting him but he resisted; they thought he had reached for his gun, and they had to shoot him. Then they saw he just had a Coke bottle.

Two days later, the second gunman, Thomas Trantino, gave himself up. His lawyer told the judge that he was afraid the cops would kill him. In due course he received a life sentence. During twenty years in prison he reformed, found religion, educated himself, and became a model prisoner. In 1985 he was scheduled to be paroled. The friends and family of the cops and other members of the force were outraged. They insisted Trantino had crossed so far beyond the boundaries of human behavior there was no way he could ever come back; he would have to be shut away forever. They told the parole board that a criterion for parole is restitution, and the only way Trantino could make restitution was by restoring the dead to life. The board rescinded the parole. In the winter of 1988 he came up for parole again. The cops got a huge crowd of people out in the freezing cold to rally and demonstrate. Members of one family went on television and said that since Lodi they had felt sick every day of their lives, thinking about what had happened to their loved one. Jail was the only vengeance they could get, and they didn't want to relinquish one second of it. The scene at Lodi was "a sea of blood," one cop recalled at the rally. "An eye for an eye, a life for a life . . ." Trantino is still inside.

The Trantino case was one of those that made me believe my work was important, but my peers in medical school told me I would waste my life, that real doctors didn't become medical examiners. Their arguments worked like reverse psychology. When I went out at night I knew that I was doing something that mattered. And if other well-trained competent doctors avoided it, perhaps that was one more reason to go into it. The two halves of my life, the hospital and the morgue, intersected with the death of a drug addict I was treating at Bellevue.

Addicts get infections of the heart valves—endocarditis—from dirty needles. They inject bacteria or fungi which float around in the bloodstream looking for nice warm nooks and crannies to nestle in and grow. The heart valves, which are constantly opening and shutting, are among their favorite places. If they settle on the right side of the heart, they form colonies and clusters, move to the lungs, and cause abscesses; if on the left, where the aorta and mitral valves are, the clusters can break off and be carried to any part of the body, including the brain. This is what had happened to my patient. A cluster of bacteria broke off and went to his brain. He had a stroke and woke up with the right side of his body paralyzed. He told me about shooting up drugs, so I was able to figure it out. Otherwise, the condition is hard to diagnose. Most of these cases didn't survive, and he was not expected to. He needed months and months of intravenous penicillin and a lot of luck. Finally, he graduated from a wheelchair to a cane, and walked out of the hospital. It was a major triumph for me. Everyone congratulated me—I was a hero; I had beaten the odds.

I saw him again two days later, lying on a table in the ME's office. He had lost his tolerance for drugs in the hospital, mis-judged the amount, and overdosed. Treating him with penicillin hadn't been enough. We had to prevent such a thing from hap-pening in the first place. Deaths like his should be used to edu-cate people about the perils of drugs.

At some point I realized I was spending weekends and holi-days and all my free time in the ME's office. I had chances to practice other kinds of medicine—radiology, surgery, dermatol-ogy—but I didn't pursue any of them. I was working in the ME's office because it was what I liked to do. I could make a difference there. I had a vision of practicing medicine in a way that would touch the lives of thousands of people, that would improve the lot of humankind rather than just individuals. There's a Latin inscription on the marble wall of the ME's office: "Let conversa-tion cease. Let laughter flee. This is the place where death de-lights to help the living."

Without that dimension, it's just a charnel house.

3

AUTOPSY

ANATOMY AND DESTINY

AT AUTOPSY I am always aware of the capriciousness of life and the random nature of death—an explosion, and someone is in the wrong place at the wrong time; a car crash, and a few seconds earlier or later would have made all the difference. Thornton Wilder explored this idea in his novel, *The Bridge of San Luis Rey,* about five people in Peru who were precipitated into the abyss when an ancient bridge collapsed. "Why *those* five?" he asked.

Death marks the end of the physical body, but the body tells the story of its works and days at autopsy; sometimes a whole biography is there in the cast and color of blood and bone, the wounds and scars gathered in a lifetime. We can't see the last image on the retina, but we can see what was eaten, breathed, injected. The way people die is a reflection of the way they live. Barring accidents and acts of God, most people who are killed— thieves, drug addicts, adult victims of domestic violence—live in such a way that they attract violence. Most murder victims unintentionally court death by putting themselves in dangerous

situations. Those of our clientele who die of gunshot wounds frequently have old bullets inside them, from previous adventures.
Many of our suicides have old scars on their wrists from past
failures.

The rich die differently from the poor, the ignorant from the
educated. Suicide is favored by the upper classes, who turn aggression inward, against themselves; homicide is more prevalent
among the lower classes, who turn it outward, against others—
which is one reason we are so fascinated when a Jean Harris
kills. It is out of character, privilege degrading itself.

We see the way people have lived, the marks life has left on
them. In the 1950s we used to see corset lines. Older women of
good breeding died with indentations on their liver from the
constant pressure of whalebones. As far as we could tell, no
harm was done. Prostitutes have scarred fallopian tubes from
repeated bouts of gonorrhea. In men, the same scarring narrows
the lining of the urethra. Tattoos enjoy high favor among the
antisocial population. Something like one quarter of drug addicts and an amazing number of people who are murdered are
adorned with them. They are not the sentimental hearts-and-
roses kind that were so popular among sailors in World War
II. They are homemade, often designed in jail by a friend. They
have a smudged quality, and tend to be a monochromatic blue-
black—the supply of colored pigments in jail is small. "Born to
lose" and "I don't believe in friends" are popular expressions
of philosophy, and so is the bravado of "Kill me, I've never died
before," with a bullet hole through it. They are helpful in identifying people.

Every autopsy is a surprise. We never know what we'll find
inside. The human body is a machine based on chemical principles. Even knowing those principles, I feel an enormous wonder
and awe at the body and its ability to function in the face of terrible odds. So many things can be wrong, so many abnormalities
and diseases can be present, and yet we go on living. When I
was a medical student, I assisted a venerable pathologist, Dr.

Benjamin Morgan Vance, at an autopsy. The body was riddled with cancer of the pancreas. It had spread all over. I watched, fascinated by what President John Adams once called "This physical disgrace of human nature"—cells gone wild, destroying others. I marveled at how this man had been able to survive so long. Dr. Vance cut through the pancreas and showed me a bullet that was lodged in it, in the middle of the cancer. The bullet had killed the man. He had been shot in a holdup. He had more cancer than we normally see in people who die of it. It was genetics and the vagaries of the body that had kept him alive.

Deciding most causes of death is a process of exclusion. Seldom are the signs quite so obvious as they were in the time of the guillotine when Madame Defarge knitted a stitch for every head that dropped. Most of us die from a long-standing condition, one which many people have, but to which they have not succumbed. Usually, MEs choose the most likely cause and set aside the others. The choice may get us into trouble with those who have a vested interest in the death. Political, financial, and sentimental interests all have their own imperatives. This was the situation when Elvis Presley died, officially of heart disease. Elvis had had an enlarged heart for a long time. That, together with his drug habit, caused his death. But he was difficult to diagnose; it was a judgment call. After he collapsed, he was rushed to the hospital. Jerry Francisco, the Tennessee ME, supervised the autopsy and took tissue samples for toxicology. He found a pharmacopeia—codeine, barbiturates, amphetamines, and tranquilizers. None by itself was at a lethal level except for codeine, and then only for a nonaddict. Elvis was an addict. Was it the heart or the drugs that killed him? The doctor who did the autopsy thought it was drug abuse, but Francisco, who issued the death certificate, called it heart disease. Whether or not it was also a cover-up can be debated. Heart disease was a popular diagnosis with Elvis's fans. As far as Memphis is concerned, its favorite son was not a junkie and did not die a sordid death.

A few years after Elvis's death, when details of his drug capac-

ity were seeping out to the public, Geraldo Rivera consulted me
about a television exposé of how Elvis overdosed. I thought
there was room for doubt, that it was not quite so simple. Rivera
was not happy with my conclusions. He wanted a hard-edged,
no-nonsense statement that Francisco's diagnosis was a cover-
up. My opinion was too ambivalent for him; it didn't make for
good television. He found another doctor who agreed with him.

The standard American autopsy begins with a Y incision, a
cut from each shoulder to the pit of the stomach, and then a
straight line down to the pubic bone. Another incision is made
across the back of the head. When the body is sewn up and
dressed for viewing, nothing shows.

It takes about two hours to do an uncomplicated autopsy on
a person who died of a stroke or a heart attack. Bullet wounds
take longer. Mafia killings always take more time because of the
number of bullet holes. We have to check each injury to see
whether it contributed to the death.

The autopsy is the final proof that we are not all born equal.
Some people are born with wide coronary arteries. Where arteries are concerned, the bigger and wider they are, the longer the
life span. Wide arteries that are clogged with plaque still have
more space for the blood to flow through than narrow ones.
Newborn babies have already developed signs of the arterioscle-
rotic plaque they will die of sixty or seventy years later. The
plaque is a combination of cholesterol, fat, and calcium, and
looks pale yellow. George Bernard Shaw knew the secret of long
life. When asked to explain his longevity, he is said to have responded that he owed it all to choosing the right grandparents.
He lived to be ninety-four.

It is widely believed in some quarters that jogging and exercise
help to diminish plaque and prevent heart attacks, but it has
never been proved. This unwarranted assumption developed in
1958 after Clarence De Mar, "Mr. Marathon" of Boston, died
of cancer of the colon four days after his seventieth birthday.
He was autopsied, and magazines published pictures of his arter-

es, which were almost plaqueless. Doctors who jogged considered the activity to be a fountain of youth, and prescribed it for longevity. Twenty-six years later, Jim Fixx, the darling of the running crowd, put a crimp in this theory by dying at age fifty-three of a massive heart attack. He had a hereditary predisposition—his father had died at age forty-three of a heart attack. Fixx had an enlarged heart, and two of his arteries were clogged enough for bypass surgery. He had been jogging for seventeen years.

We think of the body as symmetrical—two arms, two legs, two eyes, two ears—but it isn't. The right lung is bigger. There are three lobes of lung on the right side and only two on the left, to make room for the heart. The liver presses on the right kidney, so the left kidney is bigger. The left testicle normally hangs lower than the right. If the right one hangs lower it's an abnormality caused by a tumor, an artificial testicle, or situs inversus, a condition in which everything in the body is reversed.

After seeing a lot of insides, we can usually tell if something is wrong. The normal liver has the texture and color of the calves' liver in the supermarket, but it is thicker. An alcoholic's liver looks like pâté—yellow with the fatty consistency that is so desirable in goose liver. A scarred liver indicates cirrhosis. Nodules form like roadblocks which prevent the blood from flowing through the liver. Cirrhosis is a nutritional disease. In Third World countries it is caused by starvation. In the United States, where hunger is on a different level, almost all of it comes from alcoholism, but not all alcoholics have damaged livers. Those who manage to eat decently while drinking copiously can die with a healthy liver.

The two kidneys weigh the same as the heart, about three quarters of a pound. A damaged kidney is usually smaller than it should be. Kidneys age like people. As the arteries harden, the kidneys become shriveled. Other organs also show their age. The thyroid acquires nodules, the lungs accumulate soot, the arteries harden. The ovaries, like the kidneys, become wrinkle and smaller.

Strangulation shows up in a fractured windpipe. We see hemorrhages in the neck caused by squeezing against the Adam' apple or hyoid bone, which is just above it. We also see tiny pin point hemorrhages in the whites of the eyes. Those are from burst capillaries. Strangulation allows blood into the head from the artery in back of the neck but prevents it from getting out thus raising the pressure.

The brain has a soft consistency, like firm junket. It is the onl organ that is enclosed in a rigid structure. It floats in fluid to protect it from banging against the skull. If the brain is bruised we can tell from the position of the bruise whether the perso was hit on the head or fell to the ground and struck his head on the pavement. If he was hit on the head, he has a bruise on the scalp, a fracture immediately under it, and a bruise on the brain under that. The injuries are directly beneath each other and the wound is called a coup injury. If the back of the head strikes the pavement in a fall, there is a bruise on the back of the head and a fracture under it, but the bruise on the brain will be on the front, not beneath the others. The brain's momentum drives it against the front of the skull. This is a contra-coup injury.

There are three traditional signs used to determine how long a person has been dead—algor mortis (the temperature of death), livor mortis (the color of death), and rigor mortis (the stiffness of death). They are not precise. The sooner we get to the body, the more accurate we are. Circumstances modify the numbers: heat, cold, exercise, and drugs can hasten or slow the process of decay and confuse the time and cause of death.

Rigor mortis begins to show two hours after death and takes twelve hours to peak. When the body dies, some cells live longer than others. They keep chemically active for a while, which is why we can do transplants. (Contrary to popular belief, the hair and fingernails do not continue to grow after death.) Rigor is first noticeable in the muscles of the face and eyelids, and then spreads slowly through the body to the arms and legs. The stiffness remains for twelve hours and gradually disappears. After thirty-six hours, the body becomes soft again.

Livor mortis has to do with gravity and also develops in a time sequence. It begins after the heart stops mixing the plasma and red cells together. In the eight hours after death, the red cells settle like the sediment in a bottle of wine. As they settle, red color appears on the skin beneath. It takes an hour or two for the color to become noticeable. After eight hours, the red cells break down and squeeze out of the capillaries into the body. The color then becomes permanent. If a person dies in bed lying on his back, the color would normally be found on his back. If he has lividity on the front part of his body, we know he has been moved—he may have died inconveniently in the wrong house, or he may have been murdered.

The third major sign is algor mortis. After death, when oxygen is no longer fueling the body and keeping it warm at 98.6 degrees Fahrenheit, the temperature falls by about 1 degree each hour.

The autopsy includes routine toxicology tests for common causes of death in our times—from alcohol, cocaine, barbiturates, and other drugs that people use for pleasure or to do away with themselves. There is a misconception about lethal combinations of drugs and alcohol. It is not the combination that kills, but the amount. By itself, each one can be lethal. Barbiturates slow down breathing. Taken in large enough amounts, they stop it entirely. It is surprisingly difficult to overdose on most tranquilizers. Robert McFarlane, former national security adviser, tried it with twenty or thirty Valiums, but that wasn't nearly enough. He would have had to take at least two hundred pills to kill himself. The hospital he was taken to didn't think it necessary to pump his stomach. McFarlane was never in any serious danger; he just needed twelve hours to sleep off the effects of the tranquilizer. He was perhaps doing what many failed suicides do—crying for help. (Wrist cutting is often used as a distress signal. Many people slit the small veins on the inner wrist and miss the large arteries, which are on the side where the pulse is. Bleeding is slow, and there is enough time to go to a hospital to be saved.)

Arsenic, strychnine, cyanide, curare, and other exotic poisons are often overlooked, and tests for them are too expensive to perform routinely. Rarely can we tell from the autopsy that poison is present. We are suspicious—or should be—because of the circumstances. Cyanide is easy to find if we are looking for it. Any reader of mystery stories knows that it has an odor of bitter almonds. The odor lingers even at the autopsy, but there's a catch—not everyone can smell it. The ability to smell it is genetic, and only 40 percent of the population have the right genes. For those with the wrong genes, cyanide provides two other clues—it turns the skin and blood dark scarlet, and it corrodes the stomach. Cyanide prevents oxygen from being distributed to the body. It kills by suffocation.

Of all the exotic drugs, cyanide is the one most associated with spies and international intrigue. As a suicide pill, it acts rapidly. Hermann Goering avoided hanging by chewing on one, and Gary Powers, the U-2 pilot who was shot down over the USSR, also carried one. In the end, Powers decided it was easier to face the Russians than eat the cyanide.

Mysteries seem to attach themselves to cyanide. During Watergate, a mini-conspiracy grew up around Dorothy Hunt, the wife of E. Howard Hunt, Watergate plotter, CIA man, and writer of thrillers. While trying to land at Chicago's Midway Airport, Mrs. Hunt's plane nose-dived into a row of bungalows, and she was killed in the fiery crash. At the autopsy, cyanide was found in her lungs and blood and in those of the pilot and six other passengers. The discovery gave rise to wild rumors that she had been carrying $2 million for a White House payoff, and that she was poisoned to prevent it from being delivered. The story was an invention, a symptom of the times. The cyanide was real, produced in the fire from burning plastics in the plane.

Cyanide has been put in everything from Tylenol capsules to Kool-Aid. As a gas it is the most effective poison for causing mass death. Only a few gases can kill a lot of people quickly. The air dilutes most of the others. In the Bhopal chemical disaster, it was cyanide gas that was released inadvertently; and cyanide was the active ingredient in Zyklon B, the gas used in Nazi concentration camps.

Strychnine also acts quickly, but not as fast as cyanide. Unlike cyanide, it is painful. It's like an electrical wire gone wild, with sparks going off in all directions, disrupting the orderly progression of nerve impulses. The body goes out of control and into convulsions, arching backward, and the muscles of the face contort into the unmistakable *risus sardonicus*—sardonic grin. The convulsions prevent breathing. After death the muscles relax, and we don't see any of this agony on the autopsy table. Without a toxicology report we can't tell if it's strychnine. If the victim has taken it in the form of rat poison, we see little seeds in the stomach. Rat poison looks like sunflower seeds. The seeds are coated with the poison. The first time I saw them they were in the stomach of an old woman. Her daughter, who lived with her, said she had been depressed and had had convulsions before she died. Others knew of her depression, too. I sent the police back to her apartment to find out what she had been eating. They found the seeds in a half-empty cardboard box. We weren't sure whether it was a suicide or whether she was near-sighted. It could also have been a murder. You can never be certain with a poisoning. The scene and the circumstances count just as much as the autopsy. We finally decided it was a suicide because of her depression.

Arsenic, colorless and odorless, also known as "inheritance powder," has a venerable history. In the Middle Ages, kings and princes had tasters, but if the taster was part of the plot he could take small amounts of arsenic and build up a resistance to it.

The Borgias favored it, and it is thought that Rasputin was an arsenic eater. Arsenic acts slowly. Four to seven hours after it is taken, it causes diarrhea and stomach pains. It used to be mistaken for cholera, a fairly widespread disease. It kills by dehydration, by unbalancing the ratio of salts to water in the body, and by shock. It is invisible on the autopsy table. In the eighteenth and nineteenth centuries, people baked it into cakes and fed it to their rich relatives. One London husband whose numerous rich wives died one after the other was suspected of having poisoned them. Scotland Yard exhumed their bodies and found arsenic. The man went to the gallows proclaiming his innocence, and years later, a curious student of toxicology tested the soil where the wives were buried and found that it was full of natural arsenic. The poison could well have seeped into the coffins. Did he or didn't he? the student wondered. It was too late to ask.

Curare, one of the rarer poisons, is lethal only when injected into the bloodstream, not when eaten. It paralyzes almost all the muscles, including the ones that control breathing. Edgar Allan Poe used this effect to enhance the horror of his story, "The Premature Burial," in which the victim was almost buried alive. He was paralyzed, but his mind was clear—he knew what was happening and that he couldn't call for help. Curare is undetectable except by chemical analysis. Two similar drugs—Pavulon and succinylcholine—are widely used in the operating room to decrease the amount of heavier, life-threatening anesthetics. They relax muscles. They work quickly and their paralyzing effects disappear quickly, properties which also make them ideal for murder.

In 1975, the FBI asked me to investigate a series of deaths at the veterans hospital in Ann Arbor, Michigan. The FBI has no resident medical examiner and does not usually get involved in murder—that is a matter for each state—but the hospital was on federal property. In a period of six weeks during July and August, thirty-five patients—an incredibly high number—had episodes of near-fatal cardio-pulmonary arrest. It seemed like an epidemic. All of them were on IVs.

Rescue from this temporary muscle paralysis consists of artificial respiration for a few minutes until the paralysis wears off. But it has to be done quickly. Two nurses were most proficient at it. Again and again they dashed in in the nick of time and performed valiantly. Only five patients died.

Four bodies were exhumed and autopsied. Nothing unnatural showed up, but tissues were sent to the FBI crime lab. They found Pavulon.

The patients' charts showed that one or the other of the same two Filipino nurses—Leonora Perez and Filipina Narcisco—had been on duty during every crisis. They were put on trial. The defense raised $90,000 in the Philippines and here. The Philippine government considered the trial important enough to send an observer. About twelve thousand Filipino nurses worked in the United States.

Perez and Narcisco were found guilty of poisoning six patients. The prosecution theorized that they were trying to dramatize the need for more nurses and chose this method of alerting the world. The nurses had no comment, but they had a champion who proved stronger than the U.S. system of justice. Imelda Marcos, then at the height of her powers, paid for part of the defense. Imelda claimed that the case was an extension of an unfair U.S. immigration policy and the nurses were victims; that the charge against them was trumped up to keep Filipino nurses out of the United States.

Perez and Narcisco spent less than a year in jail. Months later, the federal judge who had heard the case unexpectedly came down with a new ruling: upon further examination of the record, he realized he had permitted errors to take place. One of the assistant U.S. attorneys, for instance, had spoken to the press in a biased manner, he said. He set the guilty verdict aside and ordered a new trial. It never took place. I was told that Imelda was threatening to make trouble over the American bases in the

Philippines, and the national security took precedence over the Pavulon victims.

More obscure than curare is ricin, a vegetable poison that comes from the castor oil plant. Like arsenic, it's a masquerade poison. Its symptoms are easy to confuse with those of a viral or bacterial infection—abdominal pain, nausea, cramps, convulsions, dehydration. It irritates the intestinal tract, causing the red blood cells to break apart and preventing them from carrying oxygen to the heart and brain. Death comes from an electrolyte imbalance. Ricin made international headlines in 1978 when Georgi Markov, an important Bulgarian defector and BBC broadcaster whose news programs were beamed to Sofia, was stuck in the leg in the middle of the day on Waterloo Bridge. The mechanism was very James Bond—a platinum-and-iridium pellet tinier than a pinhead, injected through the tip of an umbrella. The killer hailed a cab and vanished. Markov lingered for four days with the undiscovered pellet in his leg, and then died. No one in the hospital knew what the illness was. It took a medical examiner from one of the British intelligence services to find the pellet and figure out which poison it was. Meanwhile, across the Channel in Paris, another Bulgarian defector, Vladimir Kostov, had had a similar run-in with an umbrella two weeks before. Kostov was ill for a few days with stiffness and fever, but he recovered. By chance, his pellet had lodged in muscle in his upper back, away from major blood vessels.

Shortly after these revelations, a Bulgarian diplomat with the UN collapsed at his East 86th Street hotel in New York. The Bulgarians thought his death might be retribution for their excesses in London and Paris. According to protocol, diplomats who die in their embassies are off limits to MEs, but they are not entirely free of restrictions. Foreigners need permission to take a dead body out of the country, and for that they need a death certificate.

I had no trouble getting into his hotel room—it was his residence, on U.S. soil. He was lying on the floor, as if he had just collapsed, and he had a bruise on his cheekbone. It looked like a typical heart-attack injury. After a heart attack we often see such bruises on the nose, chin, or cheekbones—the prominences. If you fall while you are conscious, you put your hand out instinctively to protect your face. If you collapse during a heart attack, there is no time for that. It is so quick, you can be unconscious or dead by the time you hit the floor. We took him to the ME's office with a physician-observer from the Bulgarian consulate. The consulate insisted on the observer, and I would have insisted if they hadn't. One reason for the autopsy is to anticipate and answer any questions that might arise, the main one in this case being whether or not the diplomat had been murdered.

At the postmortem we saw that his arteries were clogged with plaque and his heart was scarred, evidence of an old attack. He also had fluid in the lungs, another clue to heart disease. Nothing in the hotel room pointed to violence. The scene was innocent—the door was locked from the inside, there was no sign of a struggle, and there were no drugs. His body showed no puncture marks. We did the toxicology anyway, just in case, but found nothing.

The exotic poisons are mainly used on special occasions by people who have embarked on extraordinary enterprises. In accidents and suicides, the most common poison by far is carbon monoxide. It is one of the suffocating poisons. Almost all of the people who die in fires die of carbon monoxide inhalation. It combines with the hemoglobin in the red blood cells, preventing them from absorbing oxygen. Finding it at an autopsy is easy—the skin and blood turn cherry-pink. The color is a warning that other people may be in danger. One of my early cases was a man who had died in his Upper West Side tenement and been brought to the ME's office. His skin was cherry-pink. We interviewed the family. Yes, the father had been throwing up, the son said, and the same thing had happened to him, the son, the day before. He had gone to Presbyterian Hospital and been treated for stomach pains. He was not the only one. More than half a dozen people in this same tenement building had gone to Presbyterian to be treated for stomach pains, and two of them had died. One was an eighty-year-old man with heart disease. The other was an alcoholic. Nobody in the hospital had checked for carbon monoxide. Nobody knew that carbon monoxide turned the skin cherry-pink. We reported it to the police. During the summer, work had been done on the heating system in the basement of the building, and the flues hadn't been rehooked properly.

Technology has changed the use of these poisons and other ways of killing. There are fashions in death as well as in life. After 1952, would-be suicides could no longer turn on the gas and put their head in the oven. In that year, natural gas displaced illuminating gas (a combination of carbon monoxide and hydrogen) in American homes. It was cheaper. Natural gas is not poisonous to breathe. Since then, automobile exhaust has replaced illuminating gas and the garage the oven. Other poisons have been supplanted by barbiturates, which were not widely available until after World War II. They are used for suicide, rather than murder, as far as we know. For murder, all poisons, old or new, suffer from an inherent limitation—a primitive delivery system. The person who administers the poison—the murderer—has to be physically close to the victim.

The advent of the heavy plastic garbage bag has made it easier to dispose of dismembered bodies and has increased the number of them. In the old days, when a murderer cut up a body to get rid of it, he put the pieces in a steamer trunk and shipped it to an imaginary address in Florida. Once in Florida, the trunk sat unclaimed in the railroad office. After a few days it started leaking and began to smell, and someone noticed. Now, the danger of discovery is less. A killer can saw a body or hack it to pieces, put the pieces in four or five bags, and distribute them along the highway. No one will pay the slightest attention. People take the garbage out all the time. The plastic bags retain fibers and fingerprints, but are themselves untraceable.

Whatever the elaborations on unnatural death, the basic autopsy hasn't changed for a century, and the body reacts to injury in the same ways. Even with the latest technology, we have the same problems we have always had—how long has the body been dead? Was the baby alive when it was born? Was the victim drowned or put into the water after death? Was the death natural or unnatural?

4

HISTORY

FROM TAXMAN TO MEDICAL EXAMINER

THE OFFICE OF the coroner (once called the crowner) is first
described in 1194 during the reign of King Richard I of England.
It was an office essential to running the kingdom, the place
where death and taxes came together. The coroner was partly
a taxman, and the dead were a means of raising revenue that
might otherwise have eluded the grasp of the king. Suicides were
of particular interest. Because of the terrible stigma of suicide
and the laws against it (it was considered self-murder), families
tried to hide it from the authorities. According to the church,
a suicide could not be buried in hallowed ground, and according
to secular law, the property of a suicide was forfeit to the crown.
The coroner's office ferreted out suicides and claimed their property for the crown, acting as a sort of primitive royal insurance
company to help keep the king solvent.

The coroner is mentioned in the churchyard scene in Shake-
speare's *Hamlet,* where the gravediggers wonder how it can be
that Ophelia, who committed suicide, is being buried in hallowed ground. The first gravedigger explains: the Crowner has

ruled that Ophelia did not go to the water; the water came to her, and that made all the difference. The second one observes, "If this had not been a gentlewoman, she should have been buried out o' Christian burial."

The idea that doctors or medical knowledge could be useful in investigating death had yet to make a mark on the system. The coroner held inquests and based his decisions on common sense. His most important qualifications were loyalty to the king and social status. He was a landed aristocrat and was not paid. Presumably, he was above corruption and would have been insulted by an offer of money.

As time went on, the nobility relinquished its monopoly, and the office lost status. The coroner became a minor county officer who ranked slightly higher than dog catcher. In the early eighteenth century, he was paid twenty shillings for every inquest, Parliament having realized that the opportunity to demonstrate loyalty to the king was not a sufficient reward. At the time the office was exported to the colonies, its prestige was at a nadir in England.

In the colonies, as elsewhere, autopsies were forbidden by religion, but every so often there was an exception, in the interest of a higher good. Autopsies could be performed in Massachusetts once every four years for the purpose of teaching medical students, but the body had to belong to a criminal. The first record of an autopsy being performed in a murder investigation was in Maryland in 1665. A man named Francis Carpenter was accused of killing his servant, Samuell Yeoungman. The autopsy showed a skull fracture and hemorrhage around the brain. Carpenter had beaten Yeoungman with a club, and he died two days later. The verdict, handed down by a coroner and six jurors, none of whom was a doctor, was that Yeoungman had died because he hadn't gone to a doctor. It was not an auspicious beginning.

In the eighteenth century, the connections were becoming clearer between the way people lived and the state of their internal organs. In England, Sir Percival Pott examined men with cancer of the scrotum and found the disease confined to those who had been chimney sweeps as children, twenty years before. They practiced their trade naked, and they didn't bathe much. Sir Percival correlated the cancer with the chemicals in the soot.

In medical circles, the autopsy was becoming important both to teach and to treat disease, but in the popular mind it remained what it had always been—a ghastly punishment, the equivalent of being drawn and quartered. William Hogarth immortalized the idea of the autopsy as the ultimate torment in a sequence of panels, *Four Stages of Cruelty*. In the first, small boys are torturing dogs, cats, and a bird. In the second, one boy now grown is whipping a horse that has fallen in the street, and in the background another is beating a sheep. In the third, the central figure has progressed to slitting the throat of a girl. In the fourth, it's all over for him—he's on the autopsy table being dissected for the edification of assembled medical students. A dog is eating his entrails.

By the French Revolution, medical schools had begun to develop, and their need for cadavers was supplied by an enterprising new breed of body snatchers known as resurrectionists. Working at night, they "resurrected" the body from its earthly grave and sold it to anatomists, as Jerry Cruncher did in *A Tale of Two Cities*. Someone from the grieving family would come the next day and find that the ground had been dug up. Families were forced to hire graveyard sitters. They sat for three days, after which time there was sufficient decomposition to foil the grave robbers.

There were never enough bodies, and a thriving black market sprang up. Medical schools competed with each other to get them—the biggest and richest schools bought most of the bodies. Prices skyrocketed. At the University of Edinburgh's school of anatomy, Professor Robert Knox paid ten guineas per body, and two legendary Scottish ghouls named William Burke and William Hare saw a way to earn money. When they couldn't rob graves they suffocated the living, using a technique which came to be known as "burking"—putting a hand over the nose and mouth and sitting on the chest. It leaves no signs. Burke and Hare were found out when a medical student came to class one day and saw his girlfriend on the autopsy table. They stood trial for fifteen murders. Hare, the brains of the operation, turned king's evidence and got out in a few years. In 1829 Burke was hanged and given the ultimate punishment—he was autopsied. The children of Edinburgh perpetuated their memory in a poem:

> Burke's the butcher,
> Hare's the thief,
> Knox the man that buys the beef.

Knox continued his career as a noted anatomist.

After Burke and Hare, grave robbing peaked as a profession. In 1832 it became legal to buy unclaimed bodies. The great Victorian urge to understand and categorize everything in the whole world began changing prejudices, and more dissections were done. Coroners, however, were still ordinary local folk, untrained to do their job. A reformer, Dr. Thomas Wakley, crusaded to require coroners to be doctors, but his contemporaries, especially the coroners, were satisfied with the status quo. The unsuccessful search for Jack the Ripper in 1888 finally forced Scotland Yard to rethink the dismal state of death investigation. Murders often went unreported. The bodies were just buried. There were no death certificates, no general sense of who was dying or of what, natural or unnatural. Knowing that coroners could not be relied on to explain the cause of death, the Yard started using hospital pathologists in murder cases. They only knew about disease, but they were better than the coroners.

Things came together with the Crippen murder case, which

was not only one of the highlights of 1910, but a triumph for forensic medicine—pathology, toxicology, and the microscope combined to convict the killer.

Dr. Hawley Harvey Crippen murdered his wife of over seventeen years, Cora Turner, with an overdose of hyoscine (a drug that induces twilight sleep; today it is called scopalamine), after which he cut her apart at the joints and buried the pieces in the cellar of their house. To the Scotland Yard pathologist, Crippen's method of disposal gave him away. It was obvious that the killer knew anatomy. Not many people were aware that an entire skeleton could be disarticulated with a scalpel by cutting through the tendons that hold the joints together. But not all of Turner was there, and at first the body could not be identified. The head and arms and some of the organs were missing, and there was no way to tell the sex, or that it was really Turner. Crippen maintained that his wife was alive and the body in the basement was someone else. Turner was flamboyant and good-looking, and he thought she had run off with one of her many lovers. But there was a scar on the pelvis, and Turner's friends, who were convinced that her husband had murdered her, said she had had a hysterectomy.

The strongest evidence against Crippen was circumstantial. He had used his own name when he bought the hyoscine, and he had wrapped the parts of his wife's body in one of his pajama tops. At the trial the microscope was the main attraction. The issue was the scar. The defense claimed it was nothing but a fold in the flesh. Bernard Spilsbury, who was Scotland Yard's first full-time forensic pathologist, put some of it under the microscope and showed that it looked different from normal tissue. William Henry Willcox, the toxicologist, found hyoscine in the tissues and made crystals of it, which the jury could also look at under the microscope. It was the first time such evidence had been used in a courtroom.

It took the jury only twenty-seven minutes to find Crippen guilty. It's hard to say whether they were more impressed with the microscope or the evidence. He was hanged a month after the trial.

Across the Atlantic, forensic medicine in America was still in a backward state. In most places, coroners were politicians, nominated to balance a political ticket, like vice-presidents. New York City established the office of the medical examiner in 1914 after a series of scandals and disreputable incidents that brought discredit to the profession. Under Tammany Hall, the old coroner system had become corrupt. The coroner was paid by the body, but there were not enough of them to satisfy his income requirements. It was not unknown for him to pull a body from the river, issue a John Doe death certificate, and then throw it back again. And again. The coroner got $11.50 per body to look at it and say it was dead. For $10 he would provide aid and succor to the grieving family by declaring a suicide to be a natural death; for the grand sum of $50 he would declare an inconvenient homicide to be a natural death and ensure that no incriminating records would pop up later to embarrass the killer. In one rowdy episode, an unclaimed body was seen in the East River floating between Brooklyn and Manhattan. The coroners for each borough rowed out to the middle of the river and whacked each other with oars until one of them lost his balance and fell into the water. The winner hauled in the dead body, trussed it up, and rowed back to shore, as hundreds cheered. Such spectacles did nothing to advance the integrity of the profession, and in 1914, a reform mayor, John Purroy Mitchel, defeated Tammany, and replaced the office of coroner with that of the medical examiner. He made it a civil service job, based on merit. For the first time, the chief ME had to be a physician and a pathologist trained in doing autopsies. Applicants were required to take a written exam and perform an autopsy. In February 1918, Dr. Charles Norris, the head of Bellevue Hospital Laboratory, assumed office as the first chief ME.

The rest of the country continued the old ways. There is still no national system of death investigation in the United States.

Every state has a different method, and most don't use trained forensic pathologists. The system in each community depends on historical accident. Usually a given system has changed gradually, sometimes unavoidably, forced by events that exposed its flaws.

In Oklahoma City in the 1960s, the event was the indictment for murder of the son of a very substantial citizen. George Cole, who was in his late teens, and two of his college friends, out for fun, picked up a twenty-four-year-old man and got into a brawl with him in a parking lot. The man, John Wallace, who had two children, fell down dead. The hospital pathologist who did the autopsy diagnosed death from a brain hemorrhage caused by a punch received in the fight, which made it a homicide. He described the ruptured vessel as having an aneurysm in it. But he had misinterpreted his findings. At the trial it came out that the aneurysm had probably started to blow out before the fight, while Wallace was in a bar. He had a headache from it; he was disoriented, acting peculiarly, and he started the fight. When he fell down, it was because of the aneurysm, not the fight. He died of natural causes.

There were headlines in the newspapers, and Cole's father complained that his son had been indicted for a nonexistent murder because of an untrained pathologist. Soon, Oklahoma established an ME's office headed by a forensic pathologist, but the state shied away from funding it. The ME was forced to use the facilities at the local hospital, which infuriated the hospital's staff. Decomposing bodies came in and stank up the place. In an act of desperation, the ME autopsied one of them in the field outside the hospital to make the point that he needed more money. He got it.

Lack of money was also a problem for Dr. Norris, New York City's first chief ME. A big, imposing man with a gray Vandyke beard, Norris was a wealthy aristocrat for whom it was out of character to beg and grovel for bigger budgets. He supplemented the salaries of the doctors and secretaries on his staff with his own money. Doctors earned $2,000 to $3,000 a year.

Norris died in 1935. His successor, Thomas A. Gonzales, who was chief until 1954, had no trouble attracting doctors, even at such abysmal salaries. During the Depression, when doctors were often paid in kind, if at all, $3,000 a year looked very attractive. Later, after World War II, they were locked in by golden handcuffs—their pensions and benefits.

Milton Helpern was chief ME from 1954 to 1974. The job was easier then than now. In the early 1970s, when practically everything became politicized, MEs began to get into trouble. The public noticed when people died in police custody. Before, blacks and other minorities had few civil rights. People had always died in police custody, but there had never been regular public outcries about it, the prevailing view being that they were the bad guys and the police were the good guys. If MEs diagnosed those deaths in custody as heart failures, we enraged the families. If we said they were due to excessive force, we enraged the cops. So it was that an office that started as a twelfth-century branch of internal revenue became a center of municipal power struggles.

These days it's a rare ME who manages to stay out of trouble for any length of time and still maintain his independence. The job is an unhappy combination of science and politics, two disciplines that do not mix well, and the result is inevitably controversy. MEs are not team players. Over the years there is a buildup of cases in which the ME has been too independent to suit the tastes of the politicians, prosecutors, defense attorneys, and insurance companies. He makes enemies in powerful places. The child of an influential family dies of an overdose and the family does not want the cause on the death certificate. The wife of a politician commits suicide and the husband wants it declared a natural death. Truth is not the criterion. If we do our job right, one group of people or another will be offended, and we can become a political liability in the next election. Thomas Noguchi of Los Angeles was brought down for reasons that had nothing to do with his competence and so were two of the best MEs who served with me on the Assassinations Committee, Cyril Wecht of Pittsburgh and Werner Spitz of Detroit.

The Los Angeles County Board of Supervisors tried to fire Noguchi twice, once in 1969 for allegedly praying that two 747s would collide so he would have a lot of bodies to autopsy. After litigation he was reinstated, but in 1982 he was demoted from chief and transferred to a teaching job with higher pay. He became a professor of pathology at the University of Southern California. This lateral move took place after Noguchi made public his findings that William Holden's death was directly connected to the actor's alcoholism. Frank Sinatra and other influential friends of Holden's objected strongly. Noguchi had no right, they said. But it had always been Noguchi's policy to release the cause of death. It is a public office. Most MEs do the same.

Wecht ran for county commissioner and other political offices and antagonized a lot of politicians during his campaigns, one of whom was the sheriff of Allegheny County (which includes Pittsburgh). The sheriff investigated Wecht's coroner's office and accused him of using county facilities for outside work. Most MEs do outside work to supplement their income. Salaries run about $80,000—less than half of what pathologists generally make around the country. Wecht had been providing services quite openly to other counties at their request. He also had a private practice. In his defense, he claimed this work benefitted the county—medical students, doctors, and lawyers watched him perform the autopsies and learned from them. After the charges were raised, he ran for the U.S. Senate and was defeated. He now teaches, writes, and consults.

Spitz was forced to retire when the director of the health department charged that he was "not a team player," and dredged up a fifteen-year-old contract he had made to do autopsies in another county. The contract had previously been approved. The director also said Spitz took things from the office that did not belong to him. The list was leaked to the press, and when he left in September 1988, one newspaper story read: SPITZ STEALS PENIS. The penis in question had been kept in a jar on exhibit in the little museum attached to the ME's office. It had been put away in a closet temporarily.

My turn came, too.

5

MANHATTAN POSTMORTEM

CITY POLITICS

BECOMING THE CHIEF medical examiner of New York was a fulfillment. I had worked in the ME's office for eighteen years; I had studied and apprenticed for it. I had published, done research, taught, and testified. I had had gubernatorial and mayoral appointments, and been named to the Select Committee on Assassinations. My mentor had been one of the few qualified full-time forensic pathologists in the U.S.—Milton Helpern.

I envisioned the office as independent, scientific, apolitical. Pure. Robert Morgenthau, the district attorney of Manhattan, saw it as an arm of the DA's office, with a malleable ME doing his bidding. But if the DA needs a rape in order to prosecute, should the ME somehow find evidence consistent with a rape? If the police say their prisoner died of a heart attack and not a choke hold, should the ME oblige with a death certificate that says cardiac arrest? What is really wanted is an elastic man, one who will stretch and bend his findings to suit the DA's needs and the political climate. Truth and excellence play no part in this arrangement. Numbers are what count, getting convictions for the DA, and the ME's office exists for that purpose. Its own purposes are always subordinate to somebody else's agenda. The DA and his numbers look good for a while, but the ME is degraded and his work suffers. The office succumbs to creeping corruption, a little bit here, a little bit there, until it begins to resemble the old coroner system it replaced.

Perhaps it wasn't surprising that I lasted only a year.

I was sworn in on August 3, 1978. When I inherited the office, nine doctors were responsible for 6,500 autopsies per year. I hired eight full-time board-certified forensic pathologists (there were only about 150 of them in the whole country) and a serologist. They worked for low salaries (our budget was only $2.8 million), but the job offered psychic income, professional gratification. There was enthusiasm, interest; we had research projects going on, and medical students flocked to us. I had great plans. We were going to lead the country in a renaissance of forensic medicine.

I thought the office should be involved in environmental medicine. After all, we are public health doctors, and we had a unique opportunity to set up research programs. We were the only ones who were autopsying healthy people. The hospitals had all the sick ones. Our clients had been hit by a car or gotten into a knife fight; they were fine except that they were dead. I started to save the tissues of normal people to use as a comparison, a baseline, for future measurements. I was inspired by the mercury scare. High levels of mercury were reported to have been found in swordfish, but what had actually been found was a more accurate testing technique. New technologies set new standards, and there is nothing to compare them with. According to my measurements, the level of mercury was the same as it had always been.

A similar problem existed with radioactive contamination. In March 1979, one of the nuclear reactors at Three Mile Island almost melted down, and everyone started measuring the levels of radioactive iodine. The trouble was, nobody knew exactly what those levels had been before. Nobody had monitored the amounts normally present in people's bodies. Scientists had tested cows and milk and grass, but not people. I worked out an arrangement to collect and test tissues with Merrill Eisenbud, a professor at the Institute of Environmental Medicine at New York University, and Richard Coumbis, New Jersey's chief toxicologist. New Jersey has an inordinate number of cancer cases for its population. We planned to get a big freezer and stock it with specimens—livers, bone marrow, and blood—to find out the normal levels of radioactive iodine or strontium or PCBs or dioxin. I thought our freezer would serve as an early-warning system. I saw the office as a place of life, where the living could benefit from our knowledge.

At the end of my first year, on the morning of Friday, July 13, 1979 (my daughter's birthday), I supervised the autopsy of Carmine Galante, the Mafia boss who had been gunned down in a restaurant the day before, and then went to City Hall to see Mayor Koch. He was warm and friendly. My year of probation was almost over, he explained (that confused me; it was a six-month probation and it was over), and he had asked the five New York City district attorneys and my boss, Reinaldo Ferrer, the health commissioner, for letters evaluating my performance. Such letters were standard procedure, he assured me. Four of the letters were complimentary but he'd gotten two negative ones, and he wanted me to answer them so he would have my replies on file. It was just pro forma. One letter was from Ferrer; the other was from Robert Morgenthau, the Manhattan DA.

It disturbed me that Ferrer, my boss, had sent a critical letter. Only two months before, he had praised me in a speech. Morgenthau didn't worry me particularly. In my view we were not natural allies; he and I were supposed to check and balance each other. Should I talk to him? I asked Koch, thinking that the matter could be disposed of easily. Koch thought that was a terrible idea. Whatever I did, he specifically did not want me to talk to Morgenthau. The letter was confidential; he did not want Morgenthau to know he had shown it to me. My reply in writing was to be equally confidential, just for his files. I took both letters back to my office.

There were twelve complaints, four from Morgenthau and eight from Ferrer. Some criticized my administrative abilities (sloppy), others my judgment (bad), and others my attitude (uncooperative). I was also accused of mishandling five cases.

I sent two letters answering the complaints back to Koch and met with him again on July 31. Our second meeting was more formal than the first. He told me he couldn't live with a situation in which the chief medical examiner lacked the confidence of the most important district attorney in the city, and he was demoting me. I would no longer be chief. He also had a second letter from Morgenthau. He had given my confidential reply to Morgenthau's first letter (which was also confidential) to Morgenthau, and Morgenthau had answered it. Now Koch gave Morgenthau's second letter to me. It was an elaboration of his first. Koch himself wrote nothing.

Among Ferrer's administrative charges:

1. I had hired four associate MEs who sold their houses and came to New York before getting Ferrer's approval. This cost the Department of Health over $200,000 and created havoc with the budget.

I replied that I didn't have the power to hire anyone without authorization. Ferrer had approved the hiring. One of them was his neighbor in Westchester whom he had asked me to hire. No one had a house to sell.

2. He had requested but not received a detailed analysis of the structure of the MEs office.

I had sent him a seventy-page analysis.

3. It had taken me six months to review all services for which fees might be charged (such as giving a copy of the autopsy report to the family) with an eye to raising the price.

This was correct. I hadn't done it fast enough.

4. I had left the city without informing him or the mayor of my whereabouts.

This was false. I had not.

5. I had illegally requested the records of a former methadone patient from Beth Israel Hospital, violating federal laws on patient confidentiality.

We were investigating the death of a man with a ruptured spleen who could have been murdered or could have died of a preexisting disease. We requested the medical history on his spleen, not his records on drug use. Ferrer had gotten it for us.

Morgenthau had four charges altogether, two of them about my administrative techniques:

1. My office had lost two knives and a pair of pants that were evidence in a murder case.

We had indeed misplaced them. We couldn't find them for three months. "It is difficult to assess what effect the loss of the evidence will have on the trial," Morgenthau wrote. But we had found the evidence before it was needed for the trial—we had found it even before he wrote the letter.

2. I had kept Laura Drega, one of the assistant DAs, waiting for forty-five minutes, and when I finally got around to seeing her, there was another person in the room.

I had kept her waiting. The MEs office was outnumbered—there were nine of us and about two hundred assistant DAs, many unfamiliar with the ME's office. Drega was relatively inexperienced with homicide and was unfamiliar with autopsy reports. The other person in the room had been an ME who was supposed to be there.

Three years later, when I sued Koch for wrongful dismissal, Drega, who is now a judge in Brooklyn, was working for Elizabeth Holtzman, the Brooklyn DA. We subpoenaed her, but she was too busy and said she was not going to answer the summons. The judge was outraged that a lawyer would ignore a summons. He telephoned her, but she turned him down too. Finally, he sent two federal marshals to bring her in, with instructions to use handcuffs if necessary. She arrived without the handcuffs. It took us two days to get her to court in order to testify that I had kept her waiting for forty-five minutes.

The remaining five complaints charged me with mishandling five cases. Four of them had been inherited from my predecessor. They were either unfinished or had been reopened during my tenure.

People v. *Levine,* one of Morgenthau's cases, was a stabbing and strangulation death on the Lower East Side. The assistant DA wanted the ME to say it was also a rape. The killer, David Levine, had broken into a neighbor's apartment to burgle it. He thought Miriam Weinfeld, the woman who lived there, had left for work, but she was late that day; she was still in the shower, and she surprised him. She came out and found him and he killed her. Within hours of her death, Levine was caught buying things on her credit cards. The evidence against him was strong, but it was also circumstantial. Robert Warren, the assistant DA, who was on his first homicide case, thought it was a rape and also thought the jury would be more likely to convict if it was. The body was found nude and covered with a bloodstained blanket. The serology report stated that acid phosphatase was present in the vagina. Semen contains acid phosphatase, and Warren assumed this was evidence of semen. But acid phosphatase is ubiquitous. Broccoli and cabbage have large amounts of it, and so do snails. It is commonly present in the vagina. Without sperm and certain chemicals found in semen, its presence meant nothing. One other factor ruled out rape. Weinfeld was a virgin. Her hymen was intact.

The acid phosphatase disagreement had reverberations. Morgenthau accused me of having flippantly remarked to Warren and others at a conference that the victim was "putting snails up her vagina," and the snails would account for the acid phosphatase. Warren professed himself to be outraged by my vulgar utterance, although, at the time, he kept his feelings a secret. Later, at my trial, no one could be found who had heard me express this opinion, and several people who had been at the conference told television reporters that I had never said it. Warren had to back down. At the trial he took the position that I said it as we passed each other in the hallway when no one else was there. I had never said it.

Before the Levine trial, Dr. Josette Montas, the ME who had done the autopsy, asked me to have a conference with Warren to discuss the phosphatase business. She was caught between us and wanted guidance on how far she could go with saying it was rape. Could the penis have gone in maybe an inch? Half an inch? I said no, there was no sexual penetration. At Levine's trial for murder, the prosecution asked Montas if her findings were "consistent with" rape. She said yes. Levine's defense lawyer didn't have the presence of mind to ask her if her findings were also consistent with its not being rape. Levine was convicted and put away.

This sort of creative justice undermines the entire system. The important thing here is winning, and if truth and fairness are stretched in the process, so be it—it's just a slight bending of the facts, a little embellishment. Everyone knows the killer is guilty. If the ME can say the victim was raped as well as strangled, or dead for four hours instead of two, the DA will be absolutely certain to get a conviction. Otherwise, there's a chance the killer will get off. The end justifies the means. Most MEs do it, and the DA gets his conviction. But it is compromised testimony, and the lie casts a shadow on the truth.

In this instance there may have been extra pressure to stretch the truth, to correct a past mistake. It was very important that Levine be jailed. A few years before, he had been a suspect in a burglary. Levine had arranged for a friend to hold up the grocery store where he worked. The owner had a gun and shot the friend dead. The police found a note in Levine's handwriting setting up the robbery in the friend's pocket. The note was the principal evidence against him. Morgenthau's office lost the note, and the police had to let Levine go. If they hadn't lost it,

Levine would have been in jail and Miriam Weinfeld would still be alive.

Then there was the Willie Welch case. Morgenthau claimed that I had failed to provide an autopsy report for ten months, an excessively long time, which prevented his office from prosecuting the case. In their quest for the file, his staff reported dozens of unreturned phone calls, which caused much annoyance. I wrote in my letter that most of them were returned. The DA's office had no central message taker, and people never got their messages. Ten months is indeed a long time to delay issuing an autopsy report, but the delay was unavoidable and had no connection with prosecuting the case. Morgenthau didn't need the autopsy report to present the case to the grand jury. He just needed the cause of death, which he had in the death certificate.

The Welch case had begun under my predecessor, Dominick DiMaio. Willie Welch, a twenty-two-year-old black man, was found dead in his apartment on the Bowery on New Year's Eve, 1977. The body was autopsied by Dr. Yong Myon Rho, who found the cause of death to be drugs and alcohol. No one claimed the body, and Welch was buried in potter's field.

A few months later, Welch's roommate, David R. Gordon, walked into a police station, overcome with guilt, and confessed to strangling Welch. The cops found him less than convincing, but he was persistent. He confessed again and again, on the telephone and in person, compulsively, obsessively. Nobody wanted to hear it.

In September, shortly after I became chief, he began threatening to kill a cop to get attention. I didn't think a threat to kill a cop could be ignored. I looked at the autopsy records. The on-the-scene photographs were suggestive of strangulation— Willie Welch had a scarf wrapped around his neck. I thought Gordon might be telling the truth, and I ordered Welch's body exhumed.

The neck organs were in a plastic bag inside the body, as they should have been. The windpipe (the hyoid bone, just above the

Adam's apple) had been fractured. Ninety-nine percent of the time, a fractured windpipe means strangulation. I sent the autopsy report to Dr. Rho so he could reevaluate his original findings. Rho was reluctant to deal with it. He was upset. I had contradicted him. I didn't press him. That was the reason for the delay. Morgenthau won his case against Gordon anyway. I was the main witness.

The three other cases I was accused of bungling were on Reinaldo Ferrer's "poor judgment" list. One was the Robert Soman suicide. Ferrer wrote in his letter that I "was slow and unresponsive in implementing" an agreement to change a cause of death. He was misinformed. I had never agreed.

The Soman death occurred on Dominick DiMaio's watch. In May 1975, Robert Soman, a physically healthy fifty-seven-year-old man, jumped out of a twelfth-story window in the middle of the night. It was an obvious suicide. He had been depressed for months, and he had to climb over chairs to get to the window. He could not have fallen out accidentally. There was a lot of insurance. The policy provided that the family could not collect if he killed himself within two years. The two years were not up. The family hired a large and prestigious law firm and sued DiMaio to change the cause of death.

The law firm had many things to recommend it, one of them being that it had close ties to the city administration. It had been the city's counsel in an SEC investigation, and a relative of the deputy corporation counsel (one of the city's lawyers) was in the firm. I had not been informed of this. When the case was called, an unusual thing happened. No one from the corporation counsel's office appeared in court to defend the ME and his diagnosis. The hearing was rescheduled five times, and each time no one from the city appeared to defend the cause of suicide. Finally, the judge ruled that the city had defaulted and ordered the medical examiner to change the cause of death from suicide to accident. By then, a year and a half had passed, and I was the medical examiner. I did not think the court could order me to change the truth to a lie. It would be like calling a gunshot wound a stab wound. If I caved in, I would be expected to do it the next time and the next. I also thought the whole case had the appearance of a political payoff. In any event, they didn't need me. The family won by a default judgment.

Arthur Miller was another of the cases on Ferrer's "poor judgment" list. Arthur Miller was a black leader in Brooklyn who got in the way of a traffic ticket and two nervous cops. He died of a choke hold in a police car. According to Ferrer, my big mistake lay in issuing a "premature autopsy report" and changing it the next morning. "His conduct further exacerbated an understandably tense situation," Ferrer's letter said. I assume he was referring to the cause of death. Nothing else was issued. The autopsy report, which was not premature, was not changed.

Two white cops had stopped a young black man in his twenties for a traffic violation. It was early evening. While they were writing the traffic ticket, neighbors and friends started to gather around. They became a small crowd. The cops got a little flustered with all these angry black people shouting at them that they were picking on a kid. Then Arthur Miller, in his midthirties, the kid's older brother, arrived. Unknown to the cops, Miller was a hero of the community, a former amateur boxer, and a man who worked with the police to help neighborhood children. He was also licensed to carry a gun. In what may have been the most unfortunate gesture of his life, he raised his arms to calm the crowd; his jacket opened, and the nervous cops saw he had a gun in his belt. They jumped him, dragged him into the car, and drove to the precinct. When they arrived, he was dead. The cops said they thought it was a heart attack.

In a case like this—a police confrontation—any deaths have to be investigated immediately. Special care has to be taken because of the power of the authorities to cover things up. You need as objective a finding as possible, a finding that is above reproach. It fell to Dr. Milton Wald, the deputy chief ME of Brooklyn, to do the autopsy. Wald wasn't sure how to handle it; he didn't know what to do about listing the cause. We worked it out on the telephone.

"Everything is normal," he said. "I can't find a cause."

"Are there any marks on his neck?" I asked.

"Yes, bruises."

"Any hemorrhages in the eyes?"

"Yes."

"Any damage to the windpipe?"

"Yes; there are hemorrhages in the neck muscles."

"Well," I said. "Isn't this neck compression? With an arm or a nightstick?"

"You're right," he said, "but our policy is to say 'pending further study' until the commotion dies down, or to say 'psychosis with exhaustion.'"

Psychosis with exhaustion is an ME euphemism designed to exonerate the police and pacify the family and draw a polite curtain of silence over the events. It means that the person in custody started acting crazy and died while being subdued. His heart couldn't take the exertion of his psychotic behavior. That way, his death was really his own fault.

I did not think psychosis with exhaustion was the way to go. I'd been through situations like this during the 1960s, and I knew the best thing was the truth, delivered as quickly as possible, before the anger started to simmer. We would just inflame the situation by lying about it. I told Wald to say that the cause of death was compression of the neck. He did.

The Miller family didn't think they would be treated fairly. Even before we were finished with our autopsy, they hired their own pathologist to do a second one. He was very surprised to see that our cause was not psychosis with exhaustion, and he confirmed our findings. The community calmed down. Koch called to tell me what a wonderful job I'd done, and sent me a spontaneous letter of commendation. The letter later became a source of embarrassment to him when I sued the city. He had forgotten about it. Ferrer's charges said that my irresponsible behavior could have made a potentially violent situation worse. When Koch was shown the commendation he nearly fell off the witness stand, but he recovered his aplomb quickly—if Reinaldo Ferrer, his health commissioner, said he was wrong, then he had to be guided by that, Koch said.

Ferrer's last accusation, also in the "poor judgment" category, was that I publicly and indiscreetly discussed the death of Nelson Rockefeller and "included a number of details not previously presented in such fashion as to indicate that the governor had died during sexual intercourse." I was supposed to have disclosed these details during a speech titled "The Functions of the Chief Medical Examiner's Office," which I gave at Lenox Hill Hospital in the month following Rockefeller's death. My entire presentation, said Ferrer, was focused on the governor's death. Somehow, this public indiscretion remained a total secret from the media, which were slavering for details on Rockefeller's death. Not a single word of it appeared in the press.

Ferrer, who was not present during my speech, learned of it from Dr. John Finkbeiner, a Manhattan oncologist at Lenox Hill. Finkbeiner, who said he was sitting in the back of the auditorium, apparently heard something entirely different from what I said. My sole reference to Rockefeller was a response to a question from the audience. One of the Lenox Hill doctors asked if the hospital should have issued a death certificate. Should Rockefeller's death have been reported to the ME? I explained that the hospital has the right if the patient is under the care of his own doctor. If you die at home or in the hospital, and your doctor has been treating you for the disease you die of, the ME doesn't come into it at all. The hospital or the doctor signs the death certificate, and it remains a private matter. Finkbeiner's version, which he later testified to, was lengthier. He had not heard me say anything about sexual intercourse, but he said he had heard me describe the autopsy and stomach contents. He said I had told the audience that Rockefeller had eaten two meals, the remains of which were still in his stomach. Finkbeiner did not know that there is no way to count the number of meals eaten from the stomach contents. Besides, Rockefeller was never autopsied.

These charges were doubly painful to me because I had done everything I could to have Rockefeller's death dealt with properly. I had thought there should be an autopsy. He had died suddenly at night in his townhouse/office near the Museum of Modern Art. He was working on a book with his young assistant, Megan Marshak. The gossip was ferocious.

I was at a conference in San Diego at the time. The office was inundated with calls. Half the reporters in New York had suspicions to impart: that Rockefeller had really died in Marshak's apartment and was subsequently dressed and carried over to his townhouse; that this need to observe the proprieties had caused a delay in getting the ambulance and could possibly have cost him his life; that it wasn't just a scandal, a crime had been committed and covered up. Some people thought he had actually died five hours before. Part of this speculation was the Death of a Great Man Syndrome—how could Nelson Rockefeller die a natural death? He wasn't even sick; his annual checkups always described him as being healthy.

By the time I found out he was dead, the body had already been moved to the family compound in Pocantico Hills in Westchester County. The family did not believe in drawing things out. I had to decide whether there was enough information to get it back against their wishes. The funeral director was calling, requesting permission to cremate. Because of the finality of cremation, the ME in New York City, as in many other jurisdictions, must approve all cremations to make sure that nothing serious, like a murder, has been overlooked. If the body has been moved, the custom is to get the approval from the place where the death certificate was issued.

I called Rockefeller's physician, Dr. Ernest R. Esakof, who had issued the death certificate. Esakof told me that Rockefeller hadn't been as healthy as everyone thought. In the last few months he had been treating him for hypertension and heart disease. The family hadn't wanted anyone to know. The fact that Esakof was treating Rockefeller for the condition he died of— heart disease—took the case out of my jurisdiction completely. We had no legal basis to do an autopsy. Cynics thought that the family pulled strings in order to avoid one, but the family didn't have to; they had a right to their privacy. Rockefeller was not an ME's case, and he was not removed from my jurisdiction because of privilege or because he could get away with anything he wanted, even after he was dead.

Still, I thought it would be the better part of prudence to have an autopsy done. Without one, the questions would continue to be asked and the stories would never end, just because he was a Rockefeller. I told Esakof about all the calls we were getting, all the suspicions. Look at President Kennedy, I said. The more mystery there is, the more people speculate. Wouldn't Mrs. Rockefeller want to put all the questions to rest? Esakof told me that Mrs. Rockefeller had consulted with Henry Kissinger and other advisers and decided against an autopsy. By the time he called me back, the body had already been cremated.

After Koch demoted me, I sued the city for wrongful dismissal and reinstatement. The chief ME is the highest civil service position in the city, and according to the law he can be removed only for cause, such as incompetence. The mayor should not be in a position to hire and fire the chief ME at will. It interferes with the ME's ability to act independently and turns the job into a political appendage. Koch had demoted me arbitrarily, without a hearing, on the basis of two secret letters. It was like a Star Chamber proceeding. In 1982, three years after my demotion, we went to trial.

During my career, some people had racked up grievances against me, and the trial gave them a chance to cash in. One of the people who testified was John A. Keenan, a former assistant DA and a friend of Morgenthau's. Back in 1968 Keenan had asked me to omit writing "drug addict" on the death certificate of a man who had died of a gunshot wound. We had a policy about that: we made a notation on the back of the certificate, which was used to compile public health statistics. Keenan didn't want the jury to know the dead man was an addict. If he looked attractive to the jury, then the killer would look that much worse. The principle was the same as in the Levine non-rape case. It was just helping things along a little. I thought it was nonsense and said so. Keenan did not appreciate my position. Fourteen years later he went on the stand to support Morgenthau's charge that I was derelict in returning phone calls to his assistants. When he had been an assistant DA, he said, I hadn't always returned his phone calls promptly, either. In the middle of the trial, Keenan came into good fortune. While he was testifying, it was announced that he had coincidentally been elevated to judgedom. That made him a colleague of Judge Haight, who was the sitting judge at my trial.

Morgenthau's performance as a witness was marred by his embarrassment and discomfort at being there. He found himself unable to answer questions about normal procedure and the general mechanics of things, and he kept contradicting his depositions, blaming the stenographers for the discrepancies. The stenographers were furious. He didn't seem to understand how the grand jury process worked. He complained that he couldn't prosecute in the Welch case because he didn't have the autopsy report soon enough to show to the grand jury—but the grand jury is never shown the autopsy report.

Koch was his usual confident self on the witness stand. He went out of his way to praise me, saying what an excellent pathologist I was, but excellence was really not the point. "Dr. Baden's temperament was such that he couldn't work well within the system," Koch said. The main thing was that his chief ME had to get along with the most important DA in the city.

After he testified, Koch came over to shake my hand. It was just a charade after all, and no hard feelings, he seemed to be saying.

I won my case and Koch was ordered to reinstate me, but he and Elliot Gross, whom he appointed to succeed me, appealed. Gross, the former chief ME of Connecticut, had been Morgenthau's choice from the beginning, but Koch had preferred me. They won. The court adopted Koch's argument that the job of chief ME was too important a position for the mayor not to control, and that the mayor should have the right to hire and fire at will. Ironically, Koch was able to use this ruling later to fire Gross.

In 1981, I took a two-year leave of absence from New York City and worked in Suffolk County. In 1986, Governor Cuomo's director of criminal justice asked me and Lowell Levine, a forensic dentist, to organize the New York State Police Forensic Sciences Unit, to be on call and solve forensic mysteries. The majority of counties in the state had coroners, not MEs, and they needed help.

The problems with the New York City ME's office continued after I left. The Tennessee Williams diagnosis was difficult. Williams, who was seventy-two years old and a lifetime user of alcohol and barbiturates, died at the Hotel Elysée in Manhattan on February 25, 1983. Gross found a long, thin rubber medicine bottle stopper in his mouth and attributed his death to it: Williams choked on it, he said. However, it was not wide enough to stop up Williams's airway. In fact, it was not even *in* his airway. It was in his mouth. He had been drinking and had overdosed on barbiturates. The press kept calling Gross for the toxicology report, and he kept saying the work wasn't done yet. He had sent Williams's tissues to the lab under another name. The lab people knew what he had done, but they didn't know which name he had used. Gross explained that he was worried about foul play: because of Williams's celebrity, he wanted to ensure that the lab didn't leak anything to the press. This behavior was labeled cautious and discreet by some; others considered it paranoid. Six months later, after the press had lost interest, Gross quietly issued another cause of death, taking into account the secret toxicology findings—that Williams had swallowed enough barbiturates to cause death.

Another embarrassment was the Michael Stewart case, a long-drawn-out scandal with shrieking headlines which still remains a festering sore of racism. Stewart, a young black man who was caught spraying graffiti, was beaten and subdued by the transit police. He was taken to the hospital in a coma and kept alive for eleven days. The doctors noticed neck injuries when he was brought in. Gross did not identify them at the time of the autopsy.

After the autopsy, Gross held a press conference and announced that Stewart had died of cardiac arrest and that there was no evidence he had been injured. I believe this diagnosis encouraged the transit police to deny they had beaten and subdued Stewart. A few days later, the toxicology report came back from the lab. Toxicology had found alcohol in Stewart's body, and Gross blamed the death on too much alcohol. After conferring with other experts, he decided the cause was traumatic injury to the cervical vertebrae, the implication being that Stewart did it to himself, having fallen down while drunk. This is another form of psychosis with exhaustion. At the trial of the transit police, there were two competing causes of death, which meant that Morgenthau had to bring in outside MEs to clarify matters for the jury, a humiliating state of affairs for the DA of Manhattan. Dr. Brian Blackbourne, chief ME of Massachusetts, testified for Morgenthau that the cause of death was a choke hold. He was the only one to say so. Many people, including me, had believed all along that the cops had cut off Stewart's air supply with a nightstick, and he had gone into a coma from which he never recovered. (There had not been a single diagnosis of a choke hold death by cops since Arthur Miller's death in 1978.) Morgenthau lost the case. There were too many conflicting causes of death. Since then, the family has brought a civil case against the city and Gross for violating Stewart's civil rights.

These blunders culminated in the notorious preppy murder

case, in which Jennifer Levin and Robert Chambers, two children of privilege, went to Central Park in the middle of the night to have sex, and Jennifer Levin wound up dead. Chambers said he accidentally grabbed her around the neck and squeezed during rough sex. It was a complicated case, but it was assigned to a junior ME whose inexperience led her into errors and omissions. She did not search the body for fibers and hairs. She mistook bruises for bite marks on Levin and called in a dentist who agreed with her. Morgenthau held a televised press conference using the bite marks as an example of the viciousness of Chambers's attack. The marks were ordinary bruises. Levin's damp clothes were put in a plastic bag, where they acquired a coat of mold that made it impossible to use them for evidence or for the lab to do blood, semen, and saliva tests. The ME work was so careless that Morgenthau again had to pay outside experts to testify for him. This time Werner Spitz, chief ME of Detroit, came. It cost the city almost fifteen thousand dollars.

Chambers pled guilty to first-degree manslaughter and got five to fifteen years, but it was a plea bargain, incorporating other charges of burglary and fraud. Five to fifteen is what he might have gotten for only one of the other charges.

For whatever reason, Morgenthau was just as unhappy with Gross as he had been with me. Gross suffered a similar fate to mine—Koch fired him in 1987. Ironically, a few months later, an assistant DA in Morgenthau's office called me in as a consultant on the Carl Andre–Ana Mendieta defenestration case.

They were both sculptors. Andre, at fifty, was well established; his thirty-six-year-old wife, Ana Mendieta, was on her way up. The marriage was in trouble. He was a womanizer, and she was gathering evidence for a divorce. He was brawny; she was tiny. They were both heavy drinkers and fiercely temperamental. She went out the window and landed on the roof of a grocery, thirty-two floors below their Greenwich Village apartment, at about 5:30 A.M. A doorman thought he heard someone crying, "No, no, no, no," followed by a loud crash. The police labeled it a homicide rather than a suicide or an accident. They had no confession, no eyewitnesses, and no other real evidence. The ME confirmed what the cops told him. The DA, however, assumed the ME had independent medical evidence to support his findings. Even the police thought the ME had something more, something of his own to add, when he agreed with them. He didn't. Apparently, he just adopted their version. Nobody from the ME's office visited the scene. There was blood under Mendieta's fingernails and a scratch on Andre's face. Did she scratch him? No one knows. When they moved the body, they didn't protect her hands.

The autopsy established that Mendieta was alive when she went out the window. A body bleeds more if it is alive on impact, and she had inhaled blood into her lungs. Beyond that, very little could be proved. Was it suicide? Suicide does not come out of a vacuum. There are red flares in advance. Mendieta had no history of suicide attempts. Did she fall? Was she pushed? The injuries are the same if you jump, fall, or are pushed. On the other hand, if she jumped or was pushed she would have landed at different distances from the building. In an accidental fall, the body is usually nearer the wall. Mendieta's body was found fifteen feet away from the side of the building, more consistent with a jump. There was no evidence of a struggle in the apartment near the window. But finally, it was impossible to say what the manner of death was. There just wasn't enough information.

After the ME called it a homicide, the DA's office decided to bring a case, but they had very little evidence. Andre was acquitted. His wife's relatives and friends are still convinced that he threw her out the window.

6

EARTHLY REMAINS

IDENTIFYING THE DEAD

THERE ARE ONLY so many ways to identify a body. The great majority are identified visually, by family members. Failing that, the best, most effective way is also the simplest: by comparing X rays of bones or dental records to the body. In a tragedy such as the *Challenger* explosion, the Air Force had provided another way to identify some of the astronauts. The Air Force keeps a record of footprints and it had those of the four astronauts who were in the service. Flyers wear thick shoes that give extra protection to the feet in a crash or a fire. Even if feet are sheared off, they can be reunited with the right body by toxicology and immunology tests.

Even without the footprints, identifying the astronauts was easy. There were only seven of them, and each differed in age, sex, or race from the others. Everyone knew who they were. Two were women and five were men. One of the men was black and one was Oriental. The capsule they were in broke apart on impact with the water. It was found two hundred feet down with four bodies still in it. Two other bodies were nearby, but the sev-

enth had vanished. Days later, when the searchers were about
to give up, they finally found it. They hooked a long chain between two scallop boats and ran the chain along the bottom of
the sea. The remains were well preserved. They were far below
the sun line, where there are no bacteria and no algae.

In wars and mass disasters, identification is not always so
easy.

In the summer of 1985, the Army released the remains of
Lieutenant Colonel Thomas T. Hart, who had been missing
since December 21, 1972. He had been one of fourteen men in
an AC-130 shot down over Pakse, Laos. The site, the first one
the Laotian government had permitted Americans to excavate,
was known to the Army, which has a list of all the places where
planes went down during the Vietnam War. Ann Hart, the
pilot's widow, who lived in Pensacola, Florida, had gone to visit
the site with a delegation of families of the missing in 1982. She
had seen pieces of bone scattered around, and had even picked
up a humerus (armbone) fragment. Looking at all these chips
and at the destroyed plane strewn across the landscape, she was
convinced that her husband was dead. He could not have survived the crash.

The bones were gathered up and identified at the Central
Identification Laboratory of Hawaii (CILHI), one of three military mortuaries in the United States. Remains from Asia are sent
there. In 1985, CILHI issued death certificates. Mrs. Hart was
not at all certain she could trust the identification. Before accepting the remains, she wanted an anthropologist to look at them.
Dr. Michel Charney, a forensic anthropologist at Colorado State
University, looked inside the casket and saw little bits and
pieces, bone chips and fragments, that could have been almost
anything. Among them was the humerus fragment Hart had
picked up. Charney said there was no way anyone could be identified from those chips. Hart started a lawsuit against the U.S.
government.

Meanwhile, in Oklahoma City, a similar story was unfolding. Major Hugh Fanning and his electronics warfare officer (or gunner) were shot down over North Vietnam in their two-seater fighter plane on October 31, 1967. The Vietnamese returned the remains as if they were a single person. CILHI opened the pouch and saw that it contained a mixture. All the teeth matched the gunner's dental records. But CILHI also assigned some of the other remains to Fanning. Considering the circumstances of the death and the site of the crash, it was reasonable to do so. The fractures on all the bones looked like the kind of high-impact injury that comes from a plane crash.

Katherine Fanning, the widow, had doubts about the procedure. After all this time, how could anyone tell her that her husband's remains were indeed her husband's? She asked the Marine major who was the case officer assigned to help the family through the system. The major, in an effort to put her mind at ease, fudged. He said it was a dental identification. Fanning was buried.

In 1985, Katherine Fanning read about the Thomas Hart case, and all her doubts revived. She requested the Pentagon to send her husband's personnel file. In the folder was a black-and-white diagram of a skeleton. The parts that were recovered were inked in. All portions of the skull and teeth were untouched. Fanning had the remains disinterred, and Clyde Snow, a forensic anthropologist, and Fred Jordan, the chief ME of Oklahoma and a forensic pathologist, looked at them. It was clear there was no biological way to identify them.

The Pentagon was exceedingly upset by this finding. CILHI investigated and concluded that the real mistake was the case officer's kindness—he had inadvertently misled Fanning. She might not have been satisfied if he had told her the identification was made on the basis of the circumstances, but it would have been true. Fanning was not appeased and sued.

MIAs and their families are sacred. They also have a powerful lobby in Congress. As the scandal and outrage grew, the Army was confronted with the necessity of having to do something about it.

The director of anthropology at CILHI was Tadao Furue, a Japanese who came to America after World War II. During the U.S. occupation of Japan, he worked at an American military base studying anthropology and doing identifications. He had a reputation for being a miracle man—he could make identifications from bones that no one else could. Furue handled the MIAs from Southeast Asia. It is slow, unrewarding work. Of 2,413 men missing and unidentified in Vietnam, over twenty-three hundred are still missing. About five hundred of these are known to have gone down in the South China Sea, and may never be recovered. Others were allegedly seen being captured alive and were never accounted for. Every so often the Laotians have permitted the U.S. to go into the jungle and excavate the site of a plane or helicopter crash. In addition to having a record of where all planes were last seen, the Army has the number on the plane's tail and the names of the crew.

Before the scandal became unmanageable, the Army called in three consultants: Ellis Kerley, a forensic anthropologist in charge of the anthropology department at the University of Maryland; Lowell Levine, the forensic dentist who would later identify Josef Mengele from his teeth; and William Maples, an anthropologist from Florida. (Maples and Kerley are part of the roving New York State police forensic unit that is codirected by Levine and me.) They reviewed Furue's work to find out how the identifications were made and were very critical. In their opinion, Furue's identifications were unsupportable. Short of witchcraft, there was no way he could produce the results he claimed. It appeared that he first looked at a downed plane's passenger list for vital statistics—names, heights, weights. He would then pick up a piece of bone and say, This is a white Caucasian male, five feet eight—and lo, there on the list was an MIA who fit that description. It was like Roald Dahl's short story "Taste," about the gentleman who was so clever at guessing the labels on wine bottles. He got it right all the time because he peeked.

Furue denied it. He explained himself very simply—first he looked at the bones in an unbiased manner, and then he looked at the list.

There are charts and formulas that were drawn up after World War II, ways to measure bones so as to determine height, weight, sex, and race. The tables establish the relationships, but in order to use them, you have to have some information to begin with. To get something you have to give something. The charts are of little value with the bone fragments that Furue was so successful with. Fragments can be assigned to a particular person only if they fit into a bigger bone or if they look the same as the skull and match the age, sex, and race.

Kerley is now Scientific Director, and Levine and Maples are permanent overseers of CILHI and sign off on each identification. In 1987 the Army invited various visiting forensic scientists to lecture and suggest ways of improving the identification process. I was one of them. When I got there I found a public relations ossuary—an exhibit for junketing politicians. In a large room, skeletal remains were spread out on ten tables. Ribs and clavicles, femora and humeri, tibiae and vertebrae were arrayed in splendid order. It was neat, clean, and unreal.

The staff was lopsided—eight anthropologists, one dentist, and no pathologist. It was clearly anthropological territory. They spent their days matching every bone against the list of the men still missing in Vietnam, but it was apparent that the only bodies being identified were the ones with teeth. For all their numerical superiority, the anthropologists were operating at a distinct disadvantage. They were missing a very important piece of equipment—an X-ray machine. The identification of bones requires comparing old X rays with new ones, looking at fracture lines, picking up the grooves and shapes that are unique, the little trabeculae (curlicues) that make up the bone structure. They didn't have the old X rays, either.

I recommended that they get an X-ray machine and add a pathologist to the team, but even so, other military procedures sometimes undercut the entire MIA operation. One policy called for shipping dental records in the same plane as their owners. If the plane crashed, the records were destroyed. In 1985, after a crash in Gander, Newfoundland, that killed 248 soldiers and burned their records, the military developed a new policy. Now, medical records are duplicated and stored in Monterey, California. When the *Stark* was hit by an Iraqi missile in the Persian Gulf in 1987, identification of the thirty-seven sailors who were killed was much simpler—there was no need to rely on the records on the ship. However, in another self-defeating policy, the Army destroys medical records and X rays after six years, which makes it almost impossible to identify the missing after that time. Military X rays used to be stored in the National Personnel Record Center in St. Louis, Missouri, but there was a fire in 1973. Eighteen million records were demolished. Since then, whenever a dead soldier's records are missing, the excuse is that they were lost in the St. Louis fire. It gives everyone an out.

In October 1988, Ann Hart and her family were awarded $632,000 for having suffered severe emotional distress. The Fanning case was still pending.

On June 24, 1975, Eastern Airlines Flight 66, from New Orleans to Rome with a stopover in New York, delayed its takeoff about fifteen minutes because a VIP, a prominent surgeon at Tulane Hospital, was late. There were high winds at JFK that day. Eight minutes before Flight 66, a Boeing 727, arrived, the pilot of an Eastern jumbo jet decided it was too risky to try to land and flew off to Newark. The next plane, a Flying Tiger DC-8, was cleared for approach to the runway, but the pilot thought the wind shifts were too unpredictable. He almost crashed. Eastern Flight 66 came in right after. The pilot decided to land. When he was about twenty feet off the ground, he got caught in the wind shear. The plane dropped suddenly, the right wing hit a light stanchion, and the plane crashed. Of 124 people on board, 113 died. Seven people were injured and four walked away unscathed. All of the survivors were sitting in the rear of the plane.

Late in the afternoon the ME's office heard about the crash on the radio. The announcement of a mass disaster is like an invitation to a party. Within an hour all roads leading to the scene are jammed, voyeurs mingling with off-duty cops—anyone with the remotest excuse converges on it. Politicians come to be interviewed. Fire engines and ambulances line up. Extra cops hang around. The terrible secret about all this activity is the looting. It is always blamed on the local population, but it is only in remote areas that they are the first on the scene. At a busy airport, the first people on the scene are those whose job it is to rescue the living and protect the bodies of the dead. At the Eastern crash, the first arrivals were the Port Authority police, the local police, and the firemen, followed by EMS, doctors, nurses, morticians, and nearby residents. The amount of looting was immense.

Regarding looting, the relatives of the dead are in an impossible position. The firemen, the police, and the local residents all rush in to try to save the living. It is very difficult to ask someone who came to resuscitate your spouse if he took her jewelry and wallet. There is no recourse and no way to accuse anyone or even prove that anything was stolen. You could say that your mother had a diamond ring that she always wore and that it was missing, but you couldn't say you had actually seen her wearing it that day, or that it hadn't come off her finger at the moment of impact.

Flight 66 was a rich flight. One survivor said that he had put $10,000 into his wife's purse that morning. The purse was found. The money was gone. Bishop Iveson Nolan of the Episcopal Diocese of New Orleans was on the plane in all his majesty, wearing the accoutrements of his office, his gold-and-amethyst ring and cross, and a gold wristwatch. The bishop's body was found intact, but his jewelry had vanished.

For the medical examiner, the main thing is to identify the bodies. The easiest way to begin is with personal property and the airline passenger list, which has a seat number for every passenger. At the untouched scene, we can see patterns of injury and the relationships of bodies to body parts, enabling us to work out exactly what happened. Arms and legs are near the torsos they belong to, and people are close to their property. But there seems to be a universal instinct at work after a plane crash, an urge to line up the bodies neatly and an illusion that doing so is helpful. After the Eastern crash the police gave each body a consecutive number, removed all valuables from the bodies, and put the wallets and jewelry into individual manila envelopes. The envelopes were sent to the police property office so that nothing could be stolen. (At this point, there was not much left. It looked like a planeload of paupers.) In the process of safeguarding the property, they removed all remaining identification from the bodies. By the time we arrived at the scene, having fought rush-hour traffic, the bodies were covered with sheets and lined up on the tarmac under a hastily constructed yellow tent.

Most crashes occur on landing or takeoff, and the impact is worst in front. First-class passengers are mangled. Those in the mid-section of the plane suffer fewer injuries. Assuming a fire has started, death is likely to be from smoke inhalation and carbon monoxide poisoning. People in the rear have the best chance of staying alive. Flight attendants, who are usually seated backward, sustain the fewest injuries. Even in first class, they are not nearly as damaged as the passengers are. The passengers suffer skull fractures and whiplash from the sudden deceleration. If the seats faced backward, people would be supported by the chair. But the FAA doesn't think there is enough evidence to turn the seats around, and the airlines don't think the public would accept it.

In a mass disaster, most people are identified from their fingerprint and dental records. Almost everyone has dental records. One of the victims was a Syrian who had grown up with nomads. Through our embassy and theirs, someone was found to go by camel to the remote village where his dentist and dental chart were. On the chart, certain teeth were missing. That was enough to make the identification.

If fingerprints and teeth fail, we try bones. The body has 209 bones, and any one of them can be used for identification. We ask the family to bring old X rays to the office, and we then take another one of the same bones in the same position. Once, hospitals kept X rays that dated back to the early 1900s, but no longer. X rays contain silver. The efforts of the Hunt brothers, Nelson and Bunker, to corner the silver market in 1979–80 pushed up the price of silver, and with it the intrinsic value of X rays. Hospitals, which are perennially short of money, emptied out their X-ray vaults.

We made a preliminary identification of the Eastern pilot and copilot from their uniforms. They had absorbed the full brunt of the crash. Livers, lungs, and hearts extruded from their bodies. The pilot's chest was crushed. The parts were like a jigsaw puzzle—I could fit them back together with the torn aorta. (I also did blood tests to prove it was the correct heart.) He had severe hardening of the coronary arteries. I asked the FAA for his records, and why he had been permitted to fly. His cardiac exams, which are required every six months, were superficial. He hadn't been given any of the stress tests which are used to pick up heart disease. His union didn't permit sophisticated cardiac analysis. Most pilots spend years achieving their position, and by the time they are ready to ferry around giant planes, they are in their fifties and sixties, the period of their peak earnings. It is also the peak period of heart disease. According to the black box, the copilot, whose heart was normal, was at the controls at the time of the crash. It is usual for them to trade places. Some pilots like to land and others like to take off. But it always haunted me—was there any special reason why the copilot was flying the plane?

In April, 1976, the headless, handless body of a woman was found floating in Greenwood Lake which borders the Appalachian Trail between New York and New Jersey. She had a peculiar gash under her left breast, and was covered with green algae.

The body was slim and athletic, so the ME who did the autopsy thought she was in her twenties. He also thought she had been dead for about three weeks. Most people who are dumped in New York are young—they are the ones who are involved in drugs and alcohol and passion and violence. The troopers put out posters and made broadcasts asking if anyone of that age was missing, but no one came forward to claim the body. After six days, two troopers, Dan Reidy (now retired) and Jimmy Curtis (now chief of security at Fort Knox) brought the body down to the city in a coffin to show me. The ME who did the autopsy was a hospital pathologist, and they thought this case was too complicated for him to handle.

He had gotten her vital statistics wrong. She was about fifty-five years old. She had the calcium deposits in her cartilage and the bone spurs on her spine that come with age, and her ovaries had atrophied. An ovary is about the size of a walnut. As it gets older, it becomes shriveled like a prune. There were band-saw cuts on the torso. Band saws are what butchers use. They leave a clean wound. The remains of a fruit-and-vegetable meal were in her stomach. As Sherlock Holmes would have divined instantly, the peculiar gash was made to remove a scar that was distinctive enough to identify her even without her head and hands.

It was the first time I had seen a green body. I scraped some algae off the torso and went to a biologist recommended by the Museum of Natural History. Under a microscope, he identified two generations of algae—fresh green from this year and dead from the year before. So the woman had been dead for at least a year and a half.

Dan Reidy reported the new description to the newspapers, and the radio stations picked it up. The next day the troopers got a call from a woman who said the body was probably her sister, Katherine Howard of Elmont, New York, and she was certain Katherine's husband had killed her. Did her sister have any distinguishing characteristics? we asked. Yes; she had a scar under her left breast. The woman hadn't seen her sister for two years. The last time they had been together they had eaten a meal of fruit and vegetables.

One phone call had established the identification and had provided a lead on the killer.

The husband, Wilbur Howard, who was in his sixties, was known by the police to be a minor criminal. He had reported his wife missing in August 1975. The police had given him a polygraph test, which he flunked, but without a body they were helpless. He lived in a big house in Nassau County and had a workbench, a band saw, a boat, and a station wagon—all the equipment he needed to murder his wife, dispose of her body, and suffer none of the consequences. The carpeting in the station wagon had stains that looked like blood, but they didn't test out. The carpeting had been washed with detergent, which chemically alters blood, so we couldn't be sure.

Wilbur Howard was very cool. He said he thought his wife had run away. There had been ill feeling between them, but that proved nothing. He had no reason to be nervous. The body was unidentifiable. We couldn't even find any X rays to prove that the torso was his wife's. But we did have feet. We disarticulated one of them, and a trooper found a podiatrist in Elmont who recognized the toes. He was 90 percent certain the foot belonged to Katherine Howard, but he had no X rays. Everything matched—the foot, the scar, the last meal, and the amount of time she had been missing—and there was nothing we could do. In frustration, Reidy asked Howard to help him close the book on it, to put a confession in his will and lock the will in his vault. When he died Reidy could close the case.

Two years later he died of a heart attack in Maine. Given his past record, the state troopers wanted to make sure he wasn't scamming for the insurance. Reidy identified the body. It was the right man. Reidy went to his lawyer to open the safe deposit box. There was no confession. The body is still officially unidentified.

Sometimes the method used to hide an identity boomerangs and becomes a means of identification. A man's body was seen floating in the Hudson River and washed up on the Jersey riverbank. Even though the border between New York and New Jersey is a line in the middle of the Hudson River, there's an old tradition that supersedes the maps. For purposes of dead bodies, the border is the high-tide line on the Jersey side. Anything washed up below it is considered to be New York City property. More often than not, it comes from New York, and we send a morgue wagon over to pick it up. If it were on the beach beyond the high-tide mark, it would be New Jersey's problem. I always had the feeling that the custom in New Jersey was to push the body back in.

This particular body had been weighted with ropes and chains, but something had broken, and the body had risen to the surface. All but one of the fingertips—an index finger—had been destroyed by decomposition, and the remaining finger was charred. Fire acts in a peculiar way. It destroys, but it also preserves, the way tanning leather preserves the skin. The prints on the finger were still clear, but one fingerprint by itself was not enough to make an identification. There was no way to tell the man's race from the color of his skin—after we die, we all turn black—but the hair was Caucasian. From the extent that his molars were ground down, the man appeared to be in his sixties. The only other thing I found was a badly healed fracture of the right hip.

I had the body of a white male, five feet ten, 160 pounds, with a bad hip. The bad hip suggested a limp, and the missing persons bureau in New Jersey had a report of a lost husband with a limp. The wife told us he had fractured his hip in Leavenworth Prison twenty-five years before, and after that it was easy. Leavenworth had an X ray. It was the same person, and he was an upper-echelon mafioso. (We had thought he might be, from the ropes and chains. The Mafia is very predictable.) We got his finger-prints from Washington for the final identification. His one print matched.

In May 1979, a woman's leg came in from the Hudson River. It was shaved and had well-manicured toes. A few days later, I was giving a lecture and one of the people attending it, a detective from Toms River, New Jersey, mentioned that he'd had a torso for three months and couldn't identify it—it was a young woman who was wearing underpants that had strands of hair on them. The hair belonged to a number of different people. We don't see many dismembered young women in New York. There was a strong possibility that it was the same person.

We yielded jurisdiction. By tradition, whoever has the heart gets the rest of the body. The cut end of bone on the leg matched the irregularly cut part on the torso. Both pieces seemed to be equally decomposed. It turned out to be Theresa Ferrara, one of the people who had been involved in the $8.5 million Luft-hansa heist at JFK airport. She was a hairdresser. That's where the hair had come from.

7

TIME OF DEATH

BIOLOGICAL CLOCKS

ALGOR, RIGOR, AND livor mortis, the three cardinal signs that have traditionally pointed to the time of death, do not always perform precisely for us. The circumstances surrounding the death, the environment, whether it was hot or cold, whether the victim struggled or took drugs—these things can hasten or slow the process of decay and modify the numbers. Putting them all together is usually more an art than a science. Such was the case when John Belushi died in Los Angeles. Had he been alone, the exact time might not have been so important. But Cathy Smith, his Canadian friend and drug groupie, had been with him, and they were doing drugs. The time of death was critical in establishing whether Smith had given him his final injection, the one that killed him. The police investigation trailed off, which is customary in these circumstances. Deaths like Belushi's happen every day. An addict wants drugs and someone provides them. It's a consensual situation, and the provider is only technically guilty of a crime. DAs rarely go after these people. They don't have the resources. But when a case becomes notorious, they are forced by public opinion to do something. Cathy Smith forced their hand. She sold her story of the last hours of John Belushi to the *National Enquirer* for $20,000. When the police came to see her, she fled to Canada.

Belushi had been on a drug binge for four days, shooting up with Smith all around Los Angeles. On the night of March 4, 1982, he was sitting at a table at On the Rox, a bar on Sunset Boulevard, waiting for Smith. After she arrived with a bag of drugs, they shot up in the owner's private office. At about 2:00 A.M., Belushi, Smith, and a friend, Nelson Lyons, left for Bungalow 3 at the Chateau Marmont Hotel, where Belushi was living, for a drug-shooting party. In the course of the night, Robin Williams and Robert De Niro arrived and left at different times. Shortly after 3:00 A.M. Belushi felt cold and wanted everyone out. Lyons, who was the only other person there, left. According to Smith, she gave Belushi his last injection at 3:30 A.M. It was a speedball, a combination of cocaine and heroin, to calm him. He was paranoid and agitated from his days of cocaine. He didn't know there was heroin in the injection. She was trying to bring him down, to cure a cocaine high with a heroin low, which is part of the folklore of drugs. It doesn't work. Smith and Belushi then showered, and she sat on the edge of his bed while he lay on it, talking about scripts and movie deals. He was still cold, so she turned up the heat and went into the living room. At 7:45 A.M. she heard him coughing and brought him some water. He went to sleep. At 10:15 A.M. she left him alive and sleeping and drove to a bar to bet on a horse. At 12:30 P.M. he was found dead by his exercise instructor. The Emergency Medical Service arrived at 12:35. Smith returned at 1:45.

I was called in by the Los Angeles DA to evaluate the time and cause of death. Later, I was asked to testify before the grand jury as the principal scientific witness. Dr. Thomas Noguchi, former chief coroner/ME of Los Angeles, who would normally have filled this role, had been removed from office in one of his periodic quarrels with the powers that be. The DA didn't want

to rely solely on Dr. Ronald Kornblum, the acting chief coroner
(he was since made chief), who hadn't had as much experience
with drugs as I had had in New York City. Belushi's wife, Judy
Jacklin, also asked me to investigate. After reading the *Enquirer*
article, she wanted Smith charged with her husband's death.

The autopsy report didn't point to one drug or the other as
the cause of death. Under Canadian law, giving someone drugs
is not an extraditable offense, but murder is. The Los Angeles
DA would need very persuasive evidence that Smith caused
Belushi's death before the Canadians would allow her to be ex-
tradited.

According to the EMS, police, and autopsy reports, Belushi
was found with a little stiffness around the jaw, which is where
rigor begins. EMS had difficulty placing an airway in his mouth.
Rigor would have taken an hour or two to set in, putting the
death between 10:30 and 11:30 A.M. But I couldn't rely on the
rigor by itself. Rigor sets in more rapidly if you are very active
before death. I looked at the lividity. The coroner had examined
Belushi and taken photographs of him at 4:37 P.M. The pictures
show a definite purplish color on Belushi's back (he was lying
on his back when he was found), and the skin blanched when
it was pressed. That kind of color is about right for six to eight
hours after death. In two more hours, the color would be permanent—there would be no blanching. According to the lividity,
he died between 8:30 and 10:30 A.M., earlier than the rigor
would indicate.

The coroner also took Belushi's temperature at 4:37 P.M. It
was 95 degrees. Figuring that the body temperature drops one
degree per hour after death, he would have died at about 1:00
P.M., half an hour after the exercise instructor found him dead.
Obviously, something was wrong. At 12:35, when EMS arrived,
rigor had already started. But there were reasons for the temperature reading to be off. Belushi's weight accounted for some of
the difference. He was overweight, and the amount of fat around
the body organs affects the rate of temperature loss. The thinner

you are, the faster you become cold. Belushi's body would have cooled at a slower rate than normal. Cocaine also raises the body temperature. Cocaine makes you hyperactive. If you are taking a lot of it, you are wired; the muscles shiver and quiver. Belushi's temperature may have started out as high as 100 or so, a little higher than the 98.6 degrees that all our calculations derive from. From his temperature, he couldn't have been dead before 10:30 A.M. It would have had to be lower than 95 degrees.

From the mortal signs, the time of death ranged from 8:30 A.M. to 1:00 P.M. Rigor put death at 10:30 to 11:30 A.M. Livor put it at 8:30 to 10:30, but rigor ruled out the earlier time. And so did algor. Death at 8:30 A.M. was too early for Belushi's temperature to be as high as 95 degrees by 4:37 in the afternoon. It should have been lower by then. All of the possibilities could be taken into account with a death at 10:30 A.M., give or take an hour. But what was the cause of death?

According to the autopsy report, Belushi had an enlarged heart and a swollen and heavy brain that weighed about 1,620 grams. Fourteen hundred grams is normal (about three pounds). It is common in a drug overdose for the brain to have more fluid in it than usual, but this condition is not enough by itself to cause death. The effects of the drugs were unmistakeable, however, and there was no other cause to compete with them. Toxicology found very large amounts of cocaine in Belushi's organs and a level of morphine (the breakdown product of heroin) in his bloodstream that was beyond lethal. He had enough of both drugs in him to kill two people. But which one actually killed him? The physiological signs of a heroin overdose were there: fluid in the lungs and froth in the windpipe, mouth, and nose (the airways). In a sense, a heroin overdose is a drowning from fluid that has seeped out of the blood vessels. A cocaine overdose doesn't have those effects. Death from cocaine is uncommon. When it does kill, it kills by causing arrhythmia—the heart stops and starts periodically, or it beats too fast. Either way, blood isn't pumped to the rest of the body. Cocaine kills quickly, within half an hour. Many of the cocaine deaths that I have seen were brought on by swallowing large amounts of it while the police were breaking down the door to the apartment, or by smuggling it internally. Coke mules swallow little condom balloons to get the stuff into the country. If the balloons break or leak en route, one or two grams is enough to cause death.

Heroin is the opposite of cocaine. Death from a heroin overdose comes on gradually. Heroin depresses the brain so much that the brain forgets to give the signal to breathe. Within the hour you lapse into a coma and remain unconscious, going into a deeper and deeper coma. When the coroner examined Belushi, he still had more than twice a lethal level of morphine, the breakdown product, in his blood. (Heroin is a mixture of morphine and acetic acid, which is one of the components of aspirin.) Given that amount, Belushi would have died within two hours of being injected. If Smith's 3:30 A.M. speedball injection was the final one, Belushi would most probably have been dead by 5:30 A.M. Yet, Smith said he was alive and talking at 7:45 A.M., and none of the cardinal signs squared with death at such an early hour. The signs placed his death close to 10:30 A.M. (give or take an hour). There had to be a later injection, and it had to have been given to him at about 8:30 A.M. in order for those signs to start developing at 10:30 A.M. By her own word, Smith was still in the room with Belushi at 8:30 A.M. She didn't leave for the bar to place a bet until 10:15 A.M.

Smith told a second story to the police, changing some of the times in her *National Enquirer* story. She told the police that Belushi had taken a shower at about 6:30 A.M. (not after the 3:30 A.M. injection), and that at 9:30 (not 7:45) she gave him a glass of water. Her second story confirmed that the 3:30 A.M. injection was not the last one and could not have caused the coma. If you are slipping into a coma, you don't take a break for a shower and then slip back into it. If the 3:30 injection didn't contain enough heroin to cause Belushi's death, there certainly wasn't enough to put him back to sleep after the shower. Once he was awake and moving around, the drug would begin to wear off.

One last sign completed the picture of a heroin overdose. At the postmortem, there were 750 cubic centimeters of urine in Belushi's bladder (1000 cc is a little more than a quart). That much urine produces a very distended bladder. Our bodies make 1-2 cc a minute. Belushi hadn't urinated for hours. A person who was sleeping normally would have felt uncomfortable, but a person in a coma wouldn't have known he was uncomfortable.

Smith would not admit to giving Belushi an injection after 3:30 A.M., but the medical evidence was against her. So was the fact that no one else was in the bungalow with Belushi at the time the later injection was given. She served fifteen months in jail for involuntary manslaughter. She got out on March 17, 1988, and returned to Canada.

On September 20, 1977, the day he disappeared, Pinchos Jaroslawicz had a business appointment with two Israelis, Shlomo Tal and Pinhas Balabin. Jaroslawicz was a diamond cutter who worked in the block-long diamond district on West 47th Street, between Fifth and Sixth avenues. He was seen walking into the building where Tal had his small office-workroom just down the block from his own, and knocking on the office door. Nobody saw him leave. He didn't come home for dinner that night or the night after. Half a million dollars' worth of small diamonds vanished with him.

On West 47th Street they worried that his disappearance was part of a plot to destroy the diamond business along with the Hasidic Jews who ran it. There had been other episodes, other disappearances and murders. Since the beginning of the year, $3.5 million worth of jewelry and stones had been stolen in sixteen robberies. There was a Puerto Rican connection—three diamond merchants had been killed there, and a courier had run off to San Juan carrying stolen diamonds. Only a few days before, a missing diamond merchant had been found in the East

River. From the X rays of his stomach, it looked as if he had swallowed a packet of diamonds. And now Pinchos Jaroslawicz was missing. An Orthodox Jew, he dressed in a black frock coat and hat and wore a beard and ringlets. He was well known and respected in the community, a family man with a two-year-old daughter. No one had a word to say against him. But he was gone, and so were the diamonds. Was he as upstanding as he seemed to be?

The diamond business was more than just buying and selling stones—it was a way of life, a culture, built on trust. Millions of dollars in stones changed hands every day without anyone asking for a receipt. The community had an unwritten rule about guns. No one carried them. Buyers and sellers did business on a handshake, not even bothering to write itemized lists of the stones they traded in. This trust eased the flow of diamonds around the world, and it was being threatened. Was this another Puerto Rico courier case? Was there a gang of thieves killing couriers for their diamonds? What would happen to the trust? Without it, everything would be destroyed.

The police searched Tal's workroom several times and found nothing. Balabin, who had his own office, claimed ignorance. The police put out an international alert for Pinchos Jaroslawicz. By now he could be anywhere. A week later, two cops saw a 1972 Buick station wagon parked at the edge of the Grand Central Parkway in Forest Hills, Queens. They banged on the window and found Tal curled up on the floor, asleep.

Tal had several variations of his story, but the basic line was that two masked men with guns had pushed their way into his workroom, killed Jaroslawicz by hitting him on the head with a two-by-four, and stolen the diamonds. Tal was terrified that they would kill him too, so he agreed to hide the body and keep quiet about the whole thing.

After that, it got a little murky. According to one of Tal's versions, five days after the murder the two masked men kidnapped him, drugged him, and drove him around Brooklyn, Queens, and Nassau County for three days. They spent one night at a motel. The next thing he knew, the two cops were knocking on his car window. In another version, the two men telephoned him and ordered him to meet them, and out of fear for his family, he agreed. Either way, he wound up drugged on the highway.

Tal took the police to his office, where the body was hidden in a plastic bag. Jaroslawicz, who was six feet tall and very skinny, was tied up tightly in the fetal position and folded into a very small space—a wooden, boxlike affair, two feet high, two feet wide, and three feet long. The box was under the workbench. It had no bottom.

The police were immediately suspicious of Tal's story. To begin with, his former life in Israel did not inspire confidence. He had a record of car theft, and Balabin, his partner, had one for drugs and grand and petty larceny. But aside from their checkered past, how could Jaroslawicz have been killed eight days ago? He was in excellent condition, almost as if he had just been put there. His skin was a normal color, not green and decomposing, and there was no evidence of the bacteria which cause the body to bloat. Besides, they had already searched the workroom, and no one had been there. The body had to have been brought there later.

Dr. Yong Myun Rho, deputy chief ME, was put in charge of the autopsy. He knew there would be a lot of publicity on this case, but he was unprepared for the extent and intensity of it. To Dr. Rho, a courteous and gentle man, saving face was very important. A public disagreement was unseemly, regardless of who was right. He was taken aback by the anger of the ultra-Orthodox rabbis who made no such distinctions between public and private disagreements and were more concerned with what God thought of them than with the needs of the New York City municipal establishment. The rabbis thought that Jaroslawicz had suffered enough. It was indecent to cut him up now after all he had been through; let the dead rest in peace. More important, autopsies were against their religion. They were determined not to leave without the body. They crowded into the lobby of our building and the street outside, a small army in black frock coats and beards, threatening to sue Dr. Rho if he touched the body. He was afraid they would hurt him physically, and he asked me to do the autopsy. I went outside to talk with them.

I understood their anxiety. I had been through this before. I tried to explain to them that when there is a homicide, we are mandated by law to do an autopsy. It will help to find the killer. They were not interested. They told me that Jaroslawicz's cousin, a well-known medical malpractice lawyer, would sue me if I touched Jaroslawicz. It was a delicate situation, but there were ways around it. A little diplomacy was required. Even though we were obliged to do an autopsy, they had redress. They could go to court to prevent it, and I could promise them that I wouldn't do anything until they got a court order. This had been my approach through the years—to advise families of our legal obligations and their options, and not to appear in the role of the villain.

But there was a catch. Without an autopsy or a court order, I couldn't issue a death certificate. Not having a death certificate was a serious problem for them. According to Jewish law, the body had to be buried with no undue delay by sundown. And I knew perfectly well that there was no way they could get a court order to prevent the autopsy in that amount of time. It takes days. In fact, even if they went to court, it would be highly unlikely that a judge would issue such an order. This was a murder, after all. So a ruling would probably go against them.

To smooth ruffled feathers, there was one other suggestion I could offer—that I do the minimum autopsy required by law. The minimum autopsy required by law is a full autopsy, but there was no need to go into details. It was not that we were simply lying and disregarding their rights. There were many other cases when I compromised by making a smaller incision, not only for the rabbis but for any family requesting it. And we don't take specimens for teaching purposes from these bodies. I also promised that I would do the autopsy under strict Orthodox Jewish rules. They were very skeptical of this—what did I know of Orthodox rules?—so I told them they could have a rabbi present to watch and make sure we were not doing anything improper. The Orthodox believe that God puts you back together, but He has to have all the pieces. Not only is the autopsy disturbing; there is also the possibility that some of the blood can be lost.

Rather than wait to go to court, with the near-certainty of losing, the lawyer, Jaroslawicz's cousin, arranged for a rabbi pediatrician to watch. Rabbi doctors are more like doctors than rabbis. They think like doctors. In the autopsy room we understood each other; we had the knowledge, the rites of passage, the common bond of helping a patient, and all these things became more important than race or religion. Your identity is with your professional group, not your birth group. The rabbi doctor knew that I had to do a full autopsy. He understood what "the minimum necessary" was.

The game we had been playing was the game of saving face. The rabbi pediatrician was there to save face for the community. My job was the public health; I dealt with the rabbis over and over again, and I needed a good relationship with them—I didn't want to offend them.

For twenty years, Rabbi Edgar Gluck, the Hasidic Brooklyn Orthodox liaison, and I had been building a relationship of confidence in each other. He knew I wouldn't do an autopsy if it was unnecessary—if, for instance, the person died in an automobile accident. For the rabbis, the main purpose was to ease the family's grief and to let them know that they, the rabbis, had done the best they could. We all knew that the law was the law, that there were certain things I was bound to do. It was like a scene from an old play that we rehearsed anew each time. Gluck would negotiate about the autopsy, and we would say we had to do it. He could then tell the family that he had gotten the best compromise he could. I could tell the family that we had spoken to Gluck and we had done the minimum necessary, according to the law. We would all get what we wanted and needed. The family wanted to know they had done everything that was in their power to do. That was all God could ask of them. And if we went ahead and did the autopsy in spite of their objections, it was not their fault. They had nothing to feel guilty about. They had protested, and they had been heard.

At about noon I did the autopsy on a paper shroud so that no blood was lost. The shroud and even my gloves went back into the body. It doesn't matter if you put extra things into the body as long as you don't lose blood. God will know what belongs and what doesn't. The rabbis in their black frock coats and hats and side curls still surrounded the building like sentinels of death. Three hours later they left with the body of Pinchos Jaroslawicz, in time to bury him before sunset.

Jaroslawicz had died of suffocation, and as Tal had said, he had also been hit on the head with a two-by-four. He had a fractured skull and a bruise on his brain under the broken bone. After he was unconscious, he was put into the plastic bag and tied so that his feet were down. He had lividity on his lower legs, on the lower backs of his thighs, and on his lower abdomen. There was no sign of his having been moved, or his position changed. The lividity could only have happened the way it did if he had been in that position continuously since he died.

For someone who had been dead a week, Jaroslawicz looked very good. There was no decomposition. The critical thing was the cold. He was in a plastic bag without insulation, lying on the cold tile floor, and the temperature was the same inside as outside the bag. It was too cold for bacteria, which don't usually grow in the body when the temperature is less than 40 degrees Fahrenheit. When the body dies, two forces struggle to control it—decomposition and mummification. In the desert, mummification wins—you lose fluid and dry very rapidly, and the bacteria can't get started. In the frigid zones (or in a snowbank), the wet cold keeps the body hydrated and the bacteria out. In Tal's workroom, the plastic prevented Jaroslawicz's body from dry-ing, and the cold tiles stabilized it.

The discovery of Jaroslawicz's body was a terrible embarrass-ment for the cops. How could they have overlooked him when he was under their noses, so to speak, all the time? They were worried about the fun the press was going to have with them. The first thing they had to do was polish their image. They could think about the killer later. This wasn't just a little local mur-der—diamonds were an international business; other couriers had disappeared and police around the world had been looking for Jaroslawicz. They couldn't have overlooked him, it just wasn't possible, and the proof of his not having been there was the lack of decomposition.

Having gone that far, the next step led them straight into a logical swamp. If Jaroslawicz wasn't there, then he had to have been killed somewhere else and brought back, in which case he had been dead for only two days (the last search had been two days before). The logistics were perhaps bizarre but possible. In order to return Jaroslawicz to Tal's office, the kidnappers would have had to break into the building with the dead body, always carrying it carefully in the exact position in which it was found to preserve the lividity, and place it under the bench.

But why would anyone want to do such a crazy thing? Not only that, this sort of behavior was inconsistent with good crimi-nal practice. It made no sense for Jaroslawicz to be discovered at all. Without a body, the killers were beyond reach. But even if they were mad enough to take such a risk and lucky enough to pull it off, the existence of the body prevented them from ex-ploiting the fears on Diamond Row—that Jaroslawicz was in-volved in an international conspiracy and had absconded with the diamonds and broken the code of the street.

The police did have one point. The critical question was the time of death, and from the lividity alone there was no way to be absolutely certain that Jaroslawicz had really been dead for a week. When a body is kept cold, it can look as if it has been dead for just a day. But we had a new technique for determining the time of death—the potassium eye fluid test. The test measures changes in the level of potassium in the eye fluid. In life, there is a small amount. After death the red cells break down, and the potassium in them enters the vitreous fluid very slowly. The level rises predictably. This happens regardless of temperature. There was enough potassium in Jaroslawicz's eye fluid to account for his having been dead for eight days.

The police were not very happy with this development. They wanted us to confirm that Jaroslawicz had been there only since the last search. They didn't even want to believe that the potassium test was valid. I had to get John Coe, the chief ME in Hennepin County (which includes Minneapolis), the man who developed the technique, on the phone. Coe told the police captain that I wasn't making it up.

I asked the captain in charge of the investigation if I could talk to the cop who had looked under the bench. It turned out that nobody had looked. They had thought the space was too small. I could see why. For a big man, Jaroslawicz had been a very small bundle.

Seven months later at Tal's trial, the courtroom was filled with Hasidim, all in black, the same men who had threatened Dr. Rho and had tried to prevent the autopsy. When I finished testifying that Jaroslawicz had been hit on the head with a two-by-four and suffocated and that Tal had had the opportunity to do it, they burst into spontaneous applause. As much as they hadn't wanted me to do the autopsy, they also didn't want this SOB to get away with breaking the code. Tal was convicted and went to jail. The diamonds were never found.

The diamond district became quiet after this flare-up. The wave of robberies and murders stopped. The vanished courier who had run off to San Juan was forgotten. We analyzed the X rays of the merchant who had been found in the East River to see if he had swallowed anything. If you are carrying diamonds and someone is after you, swallowing them is the natural thing to do. Small opaque whitish spots showed up on the stomach X ray. I invited the New York State commissioner of corrections, who had come down to consult with me, to watch while I opened the stomach. If the white spots were diamonds, I wanted a witness. They weren't. They were little globs of barium. The merchant had had an esophagus problem of some kind and had taken a barium test. The diamonds were gone.

The case had an ironic postscript.

A few years later a doctor in a Queens hospital called me. A newborn baby had died of a rare disease—its bones hadn't developed properly from cartilage. The parents didn't want an autopsy—there was no reason why they should—but the doctor had visions of glory. The X rays showed strange abnormalities that had never been reported or been described in the literature. Undeveloped bones was a brand-new syndrome.

I told the doctor he might get the Nobel Prize for it, but the parents had the right to say no. It was a little more complicated, he said; the mother had taken a new kind of medication when she was pregnant, and the medication could have caused the baby's condition. It could be another thalidomide scandal. That made an autopsy legitimate, and I explained to the family that it could help other people. They agreed.

The doctor was the same rabbi pediatrician who had watched me autopsy Jaroslawicz. Now he was a treating physician. His research was sponsored by the March of Dimes Birth Defects. He was going to write a paper, and he wanted everything on that body tested for everything. The results were all negative. He was not able to connect the child's condition with the drug. He would have to do many more autopsies before he could begin to make any connections.

Very little interferes with the law of the digestive process. It is not precise to the minute (no biological process is), but within a narrow range of time it is very reliable. Within two hours of eating, 95 percent of the food has moved out of the stomach and into the small intestine. It is as elemental as rigor mortis. The process stops at death.

On November 8, 1983, the bodies of Susan Hendricks and her three children, Rebekah, Grace, and Benjamin, were found hacked to death in their house in Bloomington, Illinois. They had been chopped with an ax and sliced with a knife. Blood and gore splattered the walls and ceiling of the room the three children were in. The wife's room was less messy. She had been covered with a blanket before being hacked. The police theorized that she saw it coming and pulled up the covers. David Hendricks, the husband and father, said he had been out of the state for a few days on a business trip when it happened.

On November 3, Hendricks, the president of CASH Manufacturing, had told his secretary he was going on a sales trip to Wisconsin and neighboring states, and was planning to leave the following midnight and drive all night. Hendricks, who had an associate degree in orthotics and prosthetics, was in the back-brace business. He had patented the cruciform anterior spinal hyperextension (CASH) orthosis and ran a mail-order business selling it. His secretary later testified that she was somewhat surprised. This was the only time she could remember his mentioning a departure time, and in fact, the whole trip was a little out of the ordinary—he usually flew when covering long distances.

David and Susan, who had been married for ten years, were members of the Plymouth Brethren, a nondenominational religion of puritanical tenets. Its adherents lived unadorned lives, denying themselves the temptations of civilization. Divorce was not permitted except for reasons of adultery or abandonment. If adultery was suspected, members of the hierarchy investigated and decided on the punishment, which could be shunning or silencing or excommunication.

On the afternoon of Friday, November 4, the day David was to leave, Susan went to a baby shower and David took the children to a pizza parlor for dinner. They arrived at 6:30 P.M. and ordered a medium vegetarian pizza and a pitcher of root beer. The dough and cheese were covered with sliced mushrooms, green peppers, olives, tomatoes, and diced onions. The place was connected to an amusement area with rides and games, and the children played there before and after dinner. They ate between 7:00 and 7:15 P.M. By 9:30 P.M. they were home and in bed. Susan returned about 10:30. David told the police he kissed them all goodbye and left about midnight. He traveled through Illinois and Wisconsin and by morning he was making sales calls, some of which had a strange, dreamlike quality. He told some buyers he hadn't brought samples of his brace with him; he told others that he was on an extended vacation and just wanted to see people who were using or planning to use the brace. Later, the police found both models of his brace in his car.

David called home frequently, trying to reach Susan, but no one answered the phone. He didn't know what to think. He called neighbors and in-laws to tell them he couldn't get an answer at home, and where was Susan? No one was worried. The area they lived in was singularly free of crime. He even called the police and asked them to find out if there had been a car accident. Maybe Susan was in the hospital. The calls finally created a stir, and at 10:30 P.M. on November 8, about half an hour before he returned, neighbors and police found the bodies.

The police were suspicious of the scene. It had a staged, faked look. A chest of drawers was tipped forward and drawers were pulled out, but the frenzy of the killings did not match the neatness of the drawers. They tested for hair and blood samples and latent fingerprints of strangers, but all they found were the hand, palm, and fingerprints of David and Susan on the inside of her checkbook. There was no telling when they had been made— paper preserves prints for a long time. The handles of the ax and butcher knife, which were found with their blades neatly aligned at the foot of one of the children's beds, were wiped clean. There were no bloodstains on David, his clothes, or his car. As odd as it seems, the murderer would not necessarily have been spattered with blood. The body bleeds surprisingly little from the first blow. When the ax hit the head, the blood seeped into the mattress. There are no major arteries in the head and therefore no gushing fountain. The mess comes from "flyers"—blood and tissue are flung on the walls and ceiling as the weapon is waved around for the next blow and the next. If the murderer did get bloody, he could easily have showered and disposed of his clothes along the highway.

David did not go into the house. He was taken to a neighbor's, where the police questioned him for a little over an hour, and then to the station house for more questioning. The next evening a reporter asked him whether the house had been burglarized, and he replied, "They [the police] said that some things looked like some things were taken." But his remark only deepened the suspicions of the police. None of them could remember saying any such thing. How could he know the scene was suggestive of burglary unless he had set it himself? No evidence supported an alien axman theory. They needed evidence to break his alibi, something that would prove he was in the house at the time of the murders.

I was asked to go over the reports and look at the stomach contents.

The children had finished eating at 7:15 P.M. The food should have been digested by 9:15 P.M., two hours later, but the vegetables looked freshly eaten. Digestion of the onions and mushrooms had not yet begun. All of the samples were the same, without eccentricities. Not only the amount of food, but the condition of it was the same for all of them. They all had died at about the same time, and it had to have happened shortly after they got home, less than two hours after eating. This put their father on the spot. (As he learned more about the digestive process, David changed his story slightly, moving his time of departure back toward 11 P.M. The earlier he left, the less likely it was that he could have killed the children, but he couldn't make

it early enough.) If the children had been alive at 11:30 P.M.—
the time David said he left—or even 10:30, when Susan returned, the pizza would have been completely digested. Susan's
stomach contents—crudités, cheese, crackers, and cookies—
were also undigested. None of them was alive at 11:30.

The DA was convinced, and during the investigation he found
a motive—a crisis of faith. David's growing sexual needs clashed
with the constrictions of his marriage and religion. He was trying to create a new and freer life-style but could not break the
moral and emotional chains of the old one. Susan was a quiet,
unattractive, dowdy woman who wore neither jewelry nor cos-
metics. David was her match in plainness, but two years before
her death, at the time his business became successful, he changed
his appearance from an overweight, greasy-haired, ill-dressed
figure to an attractive man—he lost forty pounds, bought clothes
that fit him, and had his hair styled minus the grease. He explained the changes on purely practical grounds: he lost weight
for health reasons, and someone gave him a free coupon to get
his hair done. But the police found a parade of molested back-
brace models who had a different explanation—a story of a grad-
ual slide into temptation. The brace was designed to be worn
over clothes, but in the spring of 1981 David began telling his
models it was necessary to take off their clothes for accurate
measurements—first their tops and then everything.

He told one model that nude fittings were standard procedure.
She wore a hospital gown under the brace, open in back, and
he marked her back with a felt pen. Then she reversed the gown,
and he marked her breasts. He was perspiring and couldn't look
her in the eye, she said, and she rebuffed him. He told her he
was a good Christian, and his wife couldn't find out, and maybe
he could take her to Kentucky in his airplane.

At a convention in Phoenix he masqueraded as a doctor and
told a model to take off her leotard and bra. He started to mas-
sage her back and left breast, but she got nervous and quit. He
told another model to take off all her clothes. She wrapped her-

self in a towel and he asked her to open it. He then made marks beneath her breasts and told her she could drop the towel entirely. She had a medical problem, he said, scoliosis, a condition he could correct temporarily by massaging her spine into alignment. Later that evening they went out. He spoke of his religious conflicts. He had been reared in a very religious household and had studied the scriptures, but now he was having serious doubts about his beliefs. He also told her he had had several affairs, but he thought his infidelity was harmless as long as his wife did not find out. Driving back to town, they stopped to admire the lights of the city from a mountain overlook. He tried to kiss her, but she wasn't interested. At the hotel, he offered to pay her for the modeling and the sightseeing, but she refused. He hugged her and apologized.

At the trial, David explained his behavior by denying some of it, especially the parts about his religion and his wife (even if he was outnumbered, it was his word against the models', after all), and announcing a new development in his business—a universal brace and size chart. The body-hugging brace fittings and felt markers were part of this new idea. He had to make measurements.

Both sides spent lavishly on forensic experts. The prosecution imported four, of which I was one, and the defense called five, including Earl Rose, who had been in Dallas on November 22, 1963. He testified that there were big time variations in the breakdown of food. Those on the defense side sought to muddy the digestive waters. In their view, the digestive tract had ways and means of its own that softened the rules. As the system gurgled along, food moved through in its own good time and for its own reasons, and there were too many eccentricities for anyone to say with certainty how long it took. You could only give an estimate. Exercise in particular modified the time, and the fact that the children had been so active in the amusement area almost definitely slowed the process.

It is true that there are conditions under which the clock is disturbed. Exercise and emotional state can make a small difference—less than an hour. Certain extraordinary situations—the prolonged terror of a kidnapping or rape—would slow digestion considerably, but we were not talking about that. The fact that the digestion of all three of the children was the same confirmed their time of death beyond a 95 percent certainty. The defense was trying to emphasize the 5 percent possibility.

The jury found David guilty of murdering his family, but he appealed the verdict. He disputed the motive the prosecution attributed to him—he hadn't gone to bed with any of the models, he said, and without having been unfaithful he had no reason to kill his wife. And the surfeit of medical examiners debating the inevitability of digestion raised a reasonable doubt about the timing.

He lost the appeal.

8

CRAZY QUILT

MULTIPLE MURDERS

IN SERIAL MURDERS, the random factor inspires the most
fear—the idea of a wandering murderer, moving from community to community, unknown to all. Anonymous killers are the
most difficult to find. There are all kinds, from Jack the Ripper
to Son of Sam, and we don't really know how many of their murders are solved. They have us at another disadvantage—many
of them operate across state lines, while we are confined to our
own territory. The FBI has begun to profile the deaths by com-
puterizing the murder method and the victim's characteristics,
but catching multiple murderers still depends mainly on good
police work. Most of those who are caught know their victims,
and their methods fall into patterns. The role of the ME is to
confirm the victims—that is, to certify that they *are* victims of
a particular killer—and to find the pattern.

People didn't begin to get openly suspicious until after the
ninth child died. Before that, the doctors ascribed the deaths to
pneumonia or sudden infant death syndrome (SIDS) or an "in-

born error of metabolism," which is a euphemism for bad genes. How else could they explain so many dead children in one family?

In January 1986, shortly after Governor Cuomo announced the formation of the New York State forensic unit, Chief Richard E. Nelson of the Schenectady police department called us on our first official case. He had had a series of nine deaths over fourteen years, all children of Mary Beth and Joseph Tinning. Some of them were crib deaths, but it didn't look right to him, it felt funny, and he thought that the doctors might have made a mistake. Maybe the children had inherited some terrible genetic flaw, but what about the adopted one?

Jennifer was the first to go. Jennifer was a meningitis baby. She died in January 1972, after having lived only nine days. Meningitis is a natural cause, but the disease was older than nine days. Jennifer had been born with it, which is not a common occurrence. It is a disease that comes from bacteria—from shooting heroin with dirty needles, or from a botched self-abortion. Sympathy poured out for Mary Beth Tinning. What a terrible thing it was to lose an infant like that. At least she still had two other healthy children, Joseph, two years old, and Barbara, four years old.

Fifteen days after Jennifer's death, Mary Beth Tinning brought Joseph to the Ellis Hospital emergency room with a quilt wrapped around his head. He had suddenly stopped breathing. He'd had a seizure and suffered brain damage from lack of oxygen. The hospital kept him for ten days, thinking it was a viral infection, and discharged him with medicine to prevent further seizures. Later the same day Tinning brought Joseph back to the emergency room. The medicine did not seem to have worked; he had had a convulsion at home. He was DOA.

No autopsy was done at the hospital. The death certificate lists the cause of death as "cardiorespiratory arrest" due to a seizure disorder, which means that the heart and lungs have stopped functioning. This is what happens to all of us when we die. It is a "wastebasket diagnosis," made in the absence of any true findings.

In March, six weeks after Joseph's death, Tinning brought Barbara, her other child, to the hospital. Barbara was lethargic after a convulsion. The hospital wanted to keep her, but Tinning said no. An hour and a half later she returned with an unconscious and barely breathing child who could not be revived. Barbara was autopsied—nobody was sure what happened—and declared to have died of Reye's syndrome. Reye's syndrome, which later came to be connected to aspirin, was first described by Ralph Douglas Kenneth Reye, an Australian. The symptoms include liver enlargement and brain swelling. Barbara did not have either. Reye's syndrome is another wastebasket diagnosis. Some cause of death had to be put on the autopsy report.

In less than two months, Tinning had lost three children. She had no more left. Enormous sympathy flowed out to her. She became famous in Schenectady; people stopped her on the street to commiserate and offer condolences. She became pregnant again, and in November 1973, Timothy was born. Timothy lasted for nineteen days. Tinning found him in his crib semiconscious, blue, and making odd gurgling noises. She picked him up, but it didn't help. He was DOA at Ellis. Again no autopsy was done. The diagnosis was SIDS.

SIDS, or crib death, only happens to babies who are less than a year old. The baby stops breathing for absolutely no reason that anyone can fathom. No cause has ever been found. There are a lot of theories about it—occult viral infection, milk allergy, hormonal infections, stuffed nose. Most babies are nose breathers, and over half of crib-death babies have colds in the days preceding their death. But SIDS babies don't make noise. They don't gurgle and they don't turn blue. They are just found dead. The only known treatment for or prevention of crib death is to hold the baby. Babies that are picked up don't die.

Crib death looks a lot like suffocation, except that suffocation causes blueness. There is no damage. In suffocation, the lungs stop while the heart continues to pump the residue of oxygen in the body until it runs out. During that time—about five minutes or so—the baby can be resuscitated.

Nathan was born on March 30, 1975, fifteen months after the death of Timothy. At the age of three weeks he ran into trouble. Tinning brought him to St. Clare's Hospital in an ambulance, unconscious and cyanotic (blue). He was having difficulty breathing. Noting that there was blood around his nose and mouth, the hospital transferred him to Albany Medical Center, which is larger, newer, and technologically superior. Albany thought it was pneumonia. The doctors suggested that Tinning could use a little psychiatric help to get her through this time of trouble, but she refused. Nathan stayed in Albany for over a month and recovered. He returned home in May. In September he was gone. Tinning brought him to St. Clare's dead. She was driving the car and heard him gurgle, just as Timothy had, and he was blue. St. Clare's did an autopsy and signed Nathan out with acute pulmonary edema, which is yet another wastebasket diagnosis. Tinning was left without any babies again.

Mary Frances was born three years later, in October 1978. The following January she was brought to St. Clare's, having almost succumbed to SIDS—Tinning said she caught it just in time, picked the baby up, and did mouth-to-mouth resuscitation. Mary Frances had been lying on her back in her crib for five minutes. The doctors, completely in the dark, sent Mary Frances to Boston Children's Hospital for a workup.

After two days, Tinning signed out Mary Frances against the hospital's advice. The hospital ruled out a metabolic disorder and, failing all else, recommended an apnea monitor. An apnea monitor is a machine that is kept by the baby's bed with leads to its chest. It has an alarm that goes off if the child stops breathing. Not even the apnea monitor could save Mary Frances. On February 20, Tinning brought her to St. Clare's in an ambulance, dead. Mary Frances had been just fine until 7:15 that morning, when her mother looked in on her. At 7:30 Tinning heard the alarm going off, but by the time she got to Mary Frances's room, it was too late. Dr. Janet Christman, the pathologist who did the autopsy, found nothing. "There must be an inherited lethal lesion, probably in the heart," she wrote. She didn't test the chromosomes, but everything else had been ruled out. There was no lesion. The death certificate said SIDS. Mary Frances was four months old, the right age for it. She was number six.

Jonathan was born nine months later, in November 1979. Instead of three umbilical blood vessels—two arteries and one vein—he had only two; he was missing one artery. However, his chromosome studies were normal. St. Clare's and Boston did workups and found no congenital abnormality. On February 12, Tinning brought him to St. Clare's cyanotic and not breathing. The doctors found what they thought might be an aberration in the way his body handled urea. Five days later he was back home, but not for long. On February 20 he was readmitted in a coma. At wit's end, St. Clare's sent him to Albany Medical Center, where he lived for two more days. The autopsy was unclear about the cause of death. It was a possible pneumonia, with a question mark. It was a definite cardiorespiratory arrest.

But they still had Michael.

During this long stream of ghastly misfortune, the Tinnings had decided to adopt a child. Six babies born to them had died inexplicably, and everyone thought it was a genetic disorder. If they adopted, the jinx would be broken; there would be no question of an evil inheritance. In 1978, sympathetic agencies found Michael for them. He was eight months old. In February 1981, Tinning brought him to the hospital, vomiting after a fall. The hospital treated him for gastroenteritis and sent him home. A week later, Tinning was driving in the car with him when he was taken ill. She went to the doctor's office, sat down, and calmly waited her turn. It took about ten minutes for the doctor to get to her. She explained that something was wrong with her child, who was out in the car. The nurse ran out, but Michael was dead when she got there. Nobody blamed her.

Dr. Robert L. Sullivan, the chief ME of Schenectady, thought Michael's death might be due to pneumonia and sent tissues to the toxicology lab. He instructed the lab to "rule out suspicion of homicide." Sullivan was the first person to show suspicion. He was not suspicious enough. "Rule out" means consider the possibility, do the tests, and rule it out or not, as the case may be. Toxicology ruled out poisoning only.

Tami Lynne, Tinning's ninth child, was born in August 1985. She lived for four months before being found "unresponsive" in her crib by her mother. There was blood on the pillowcase. An autopsy was performed and the initial diagnosis was SIDS. This was the third SIDS diagnosis.

About three babies in a thousand die of crib death. The odds against two crib deaths in one family are enormous. The odds against three are astronomical. A pathologist who was consulting with the police, initially told me he thought the cause was an "inborn error of metabolism," but there is no such condition that could have affected the adopted child. There is no known genetic disease that can cause sudden death in healthy children. An "inborn error of metabolism" means an enzyme problem, and people get sick from it; they don't die suddenly from it.

Tinning herself was immune to criticism. Throughout all these devastating losses, social workers were sent to help her through her ordeal. Social workers have a conceptual problem with this kind of tragedy. They assume their role is to be an advocate for the bereaved family, not the children. After every death they came to comfort Tinning, who thrived on the attention. Instead of being questioned by the police, she got sympathy from the social workers. The doctors were equally sympathetic. All the death certificates reported natural causes. Nobody wanted to ask hard questions. Tinning became a sympathy junkie. She was the woman who lost the babies.

Through the years, a variety of causes of death were invented to take care of suspension-of-disbelief situations like this. Until 1961, when Dr. Lester Adelson, the ME of Cleveland, wrote "Slaughter of the Innocents," an article about forty-six murdered children, certain thoughts were too monstrous to think. It was not within the realm of social possibility that a parent would intentionally hurt a child, and doctors were reluctant to put in writing that such behavior existed. Instead, there were an inordinate number of deaths from vitamin deficiencies and a great many falls and unexplained accidents.

Now we have brand-new syndromes to account for the inexplicable and the unthinkable. Ondine's syndrome (or curse) is one that has to do with metabolism. (Ondine was a water nymph said to have caused the man who loved her to sleep continuously.) During sleep we take in less oxygen, and the amount of carbon dioxide in the brain rises. At a certain point, the rising level of carbon dioxide warns the brain that it is running low on oxygen and had better take a breath. In theory, in Ondine's syndrome the warning doesn't reach the brain, and it forgets to signal the body to breathe. A recently discovered syndrome is the "shaken-baby syndrome," also known as "infant whiplash syndrome," based on the fact that an infant's head is very big for its body and the neck muscles haven't developed enough to support it. Shaken-baby syndrome is a sort of death by inadvertence: the baby is shaken too hard (entirely by accident), and dies with hemorrhaging in the retina and the back of the brain. If we look carefully, we can usually see where something hard has made contact with the top of the baby's head. Even now, doctors simply don't want to believe that such things go on. Not only were the doctors and hospitals in Albany and Schenectady blind; Boston Children's Hospital, which is connected with the great teaching institution of Harvard and whose staff ought to have known better, did nothing but suggest an apnea monitor for Mary Frances, who was the second SIDS diagnosis.

MEs tend to be intimidated by the social network of SIDS organizations around the country. They have a strong lobbying group and have raised tens of millions of dollars to support research. The guilt and anguish of SIDS parents is terrible to face. They become furious if the ME asks the normal skeptical questions: Was there any plastic around? A dog bite? Suffocation? Sometimes there are accidents; it isn't really crib death. A plastic cover was left in the crib, perhaps. I've found babies under the mattress, the children of drug addicts. There's a lot of denial. SIDS organizations often try to discourage the investigation of these deaths as murders. They admit grudgingly that a real suffocation is possible occasionally, but it's not fair to disturb the other grieving parents. Smothering infants, however, is a repetitive crime. It is one of the few homicides that is repetitive, along with child battery and rape/murders.

Police Chief Nelson of Schenectady got the Tinning records for me. There had been no inquiry whatever. Each death by itself could have been explained away innocently, but not if it was viewed as part of a cluster. Two of the children, Joseph and Timothy, had not been autopsied. The police had been utterly incurious—not only had they not questioned Mary Beth and Joseph Tinning, they had never interviewed their neighbors, friends, or family. The social workers who were sent in lieu of the police found no evidence of child abuse or neglect; there was none to find.

I looked at the pattern. The death of Jennifer, the first baby, was different. All of the others had died of natural causes. She was the only one who had actually had a disease. Jennifer looked to be the victim of a coat hanger: Tinning had been trying to hasten her birth and had only succeeded in introducing meningitis. The police theorized that she wanted to deliver the baby on Christmas Day, like Jesus. She thought her father, who had died while she was pregnant, would have been pleased. Jennifer had disappointed her—she was born on December 26.

According to the records, none of the babies had been found dead in his sleep, the sine qua non of crib death. I ruled out SIDS right away. Tinning said she had picked up one child as it was turning blue, and it died in her arms—but no baby dies of SIDS while being held. The way to prevent SIDS is to pick up the child. Several of the Tinning children had turned blue—in the car, in her arms, in the crib; she brought them to the hospital cyanotic. If a baby is unconscious but alive, SIDS is ruled out. Turning blue is a sign of suffocation—the lungs stop and no oxygen reaches the cells. Nothing happened while the children were in the hospital. The single constant factor in all of these deaths was the presence of Mary Beth Tinning.

Mary Beth Tinning spent over a decade making and losing babies. During all that time the only response she got was a form of encouragement—sympathy, understanding, and compassion. That seems to be the main thing she was after. At family gatherings she considered herself the star, and she would leave in a huff if the rest of the company did not render homage. We looked for other, less frivolous motives, like insurance, but could fine none.

Tinning's husband had not escaped her lethal attentions, either. In 1974 he was rushed to the hospital with barbiturate poisoning. He was a man who did not take barbiturates. His wife admitted that she had added them to his cereal. She was having an affair with a minister at the time, and somehow could not juggle two men. But Joseph Tinning, as laid-back as his wife was strong-minded, did not feel that his marriage had been destroyed by this attempt to annihilate him, and bore his wife no ill will. He still supports her.

After the pathologist, the police, and I discussed his "inborn error of metabolism" theory, he concluded that Tami Lynne had died of suffocation, not SIDS, and a policewoman was sent to interview Tinning. She told Tinning a number of things that should have been said before, in particular that her stories were not consistent with the autopsy findings. Tinning started to confess. She confessed to the attempted murder of her husband and to smothering Tami Lynne, Timothy, and Nathan—and then it began to get late and she went to sleep. The next day, her lawyer told her not to say anything else.

After her confession, everyone—hospital staff, doctors, neighbors, social workers—came forward claiming to have been suspicious all along, but not enough to have done anything about it. Tinning had told people that her children had congenital heart defects, a reasonable story.

The Schenectady DA determined that he could charge her with Tami Lynne's death, but it was necessary to reexamine the remains of Nathan and Timothy before making a finding. We exhumed Nathan's body. It had nothing wrong with it. He was healthy but dead, a state that was in line with smothering. We ran into a little trouble at the exhumation of Timothy. There had been a mixup. The coffin contained the remains of another child. The parents had been grieving at the wrong grave. Tinning was indicted for the last death, that of Tami Lynne. She was tried, convicted, and is appealing. The rest of the case is in limbo, awaiting further developments.

The confusing thing about the .22 caliber killer (who later came to be known as the Buffalo Slasher) was his versatility. Serial murderers repeat themselves, favoring a certain weapon, a particular approach, a style. The Slasher used several weapons—guns, knives, hammers, screwdrivers—which drew attention away from his style. He left a pile of victims, all but one of them black men and that one a dark-skinned Hispanic, and that threw the police, too. Racism was the obvious inference, but the real pattern was more subtle than that.

The first killings took place on September 22 and 23, 1980. Four black men, three in Buffalo and one in Niagara Falls, were shot at close range with a sawed-off .22 caliber rifle. They had no connection with each other. The killer simply walked right up to them on the street and pulled the trigger. The gun was hidden in a brown paper bag whose purpose was also to catch the shells.

He got away clean in Buffalo, but he was almost undone in Niagara Falls. He was a stranger there, unfamiliar with the streets, and after the shooting a crowd of people started to chase him. They almost caught him, but he got away in his sister's car, driving across one of the bridges that connects Niagara Falls with Buffalo. His escape was not without a trace. As he fled, he dropped the shell casing from the bullet, a fact that was reported in newspaper accounts of the killing. The .22 caliber killer never struck again.

Two weeks later, a new orgy of violence erupted. Two black cabdrivers in Buffalo were found dead on successive nights in an isolated wooded section near the water. Their hearts had been cut out. The newspaper headlines were unnerving, although people tend to forget that in a grisly crime like this, the victim is dead before his heart is removed. But a maniac was loose, and it looked as if he had declared open season on black men. There was talk of a white conspiracy: white cops and a white DA were investigating the killings, and a white ME had done the autopsies. The ME didn't provide much information—she wasn't even sure of the weapon—and the blacks thought she was covering things up. Unfortunately, Buffalo's black chief ME, Dr. Justin Uku, was on vacation visiting his family in Nigeria. As the hysteria level rose, people began to see a nationwide conspiracy to kill black men. The Buffalo Slasher could be responsible for most of the unsolved murders of black men not only in Buffalo, Rochester (where four people were shot), and New York City, but also in Atlanta, where the entire city was hysterical over a series of child murders. Even a succession of choke hold deaths committed by the police in Los Angeles was considered part of the plot.

After the heart murders there were fears of a riot. Michael Kelly, the assistant DA in charge of homicides in Erie County, asked me to reautopsy the two cabdrivers before they were buried. It was 1980; Koch had already demoted me and in the process had unwittingly bestowed on me a reputation for being objective. After doing the postmortems, I sat down with the families. Previously, they had been ignored, and they didn't think they were getting the whole story. I explained the findings, and they were satisfied that at least a proper investigation was being done.

After the second postmortem, a picture of the killer began to emerge. One of the cabdrivers had been stabbed in the back of the head with a screwdriver, an act which requires a great deal of strength. The skull of the other cabdriver had been fractured with a small square-faced hammer. Both had been stabbed many times in front, and cut through the sternum (breastbone). There were different kinds of cuts on the bodies. Some were like stab wounds from a knife, and some—very sharp—looked as if an instrument like a linoleum cutter had been used.

In order to accomplish all this, the killer not only had to have been carrying a small hardware store, he had to know anatomy. It's not easy to remove an organ like the heart—or any organ—unless you know what you are doing. The average untrained murderer doesn't know that he has to cut laterally between the ribs to get to the chest cavity. Once there, the heart is not just sitting around in plain view; it is surrounded by a sac to protect it, and the sac has to be cut separately before the heart can be reached. This was a killer who knew. The hearts were surgically detached from their connecting blood vessels without unnecessary tearing of the sac. The procedure is to separate the ribs (not break them) and reach in blindly, knowing exactly what you will find. The choice of weapon, which combined both sharpness and heft, was knowledgeable. I thought perhaps our man was a hunter.

He also had to be endowed with enough self-confidence to go hand-to-hand with his victims. Nobody sits there and allows himself to be jabbed in the head with a screwdriver. I thought I saw a pattern. Because of his swagger, his brazenness, and his ability to work in such close quarters, I thought the .22 caliber killer was the same person as the Buffalo Slasher. Although the method was different, the killer needed the same physical assurance to walk up close to his victims and shoot them. He knew he was stronger and quicker than they and could deflect any blows they might try to deliver. The two cabdrivers were not novices, either; they knew their way around the streets, and each had an arrest record. The pattern wasn't the weapon, it was the fearlessness, the confidence in his ability to handle himself. Most murderers don't exhibit those qualities. They prefer an arm's-length relationship. They don't want their victim to be in a position to grab at them.

In December, a few days before Christmas, a series of random slashings took place in New York City. The killer ran up to people on the street (and one in the subway) and stabbed them with a knife. He killed four people that way—three black men and one dark-skinned Hispanic—all strangers to him and to each other. Two others were also stabbed, but they lived.

In Buffalo, Michael Kelly, the assistant DA who had first called me in, and Ed Cosgrove, the DA of Erie County, also thought the Buffalo killer and the New York Slasher might be the same man because of the combativeness, the bravado. Another detective, Sam Slade, considered by his colleagues to be the best homicide detective in New York State, thought that psychologically, using a knife was an upgrading in self-esteem, an escalation of personal daring. It was more courageous than a gun; it was face-to-face combat.

But this was the third shift in weapons, and no one could be certain. Slade connected the slashings and the shootings, but the cabdriver deaths were too crazy. Was this the same man who cut out hearts? I thought it was. I argued that people change methods in midstream when they have good reason to do so. Look at the Atlanta child murders—all of a sudden the victims were turning up undressed, because the killer had read that the police were getting fiber evidence from their clothes. The .22 caliber killer switched because he was afraid the police were getting too close to the gun. Why wouldn't he switch again if he felt threatened?

One way to find out more was to look at the autopsy reports of the five people who were stabbed to death in New York City. Kelly asked and was turned down. The files were locked up, unviewable, he was told by Elliot Gross. Gross refused to open them without permission from Robert Morgenthau. He didn't think there was any connection anyway, and neither did Morgenthau.

Regardless, a state trooper was dispatched to Gross's office. He was thrown out. Throwing out colleagues is simply not done. It comes under the heading of professional discourtesy. Even if it was a wild-goose chase, a sister agency had a right to see the files. Kelly and Cosgrove tried to win over a high-ranking police official, a New York City deputy chief of detectives, but he thought the connection was absurd, too. He went so far as to leak it to the press, the subtext of his story being ridicule: look at these hicks from upstate trying to get publicity; they think they can enhance their importance by associating with us. Neither the official nor the reporters mentioned that Buffalo's 75 percent rate of solved homicides is higher than New York City's 65 percent, which is below average. (The national "solve" rate is about 70 percent.)

Getting the records from the city turned into a battle of the DAs. Morgenthau got into it, echoing the upstate hick line. Cosgrove, who happened to be president of the New York State District Attorneys Association, was angered by the high-and-mighty tone and finally convinced Morgenthau to let us see the files.

Even after we had permission, the graciousness level stayed below the freezing point. Gross wouldn't let the reports out of his office. Kelly and I had to sit there and read through them under the watchful eye of his assistant MEs. He had five of them. It was almost as if they were afraid we would steal something. Gross himself sat at the head of the big conference table, bristling like a porcupine. It was very uncomfortable. At the time, I was deputy chief ME in Queens and under Gross's jurisdiction, but I was in his office under other colors, as a consultant to Buffalo and a colleague of Kelly's.

But none of this mattered. The minute I saw the photographs I knew. It was obvious that one person had done the killings. All of the New York City stabbing victims looked alike. They were young brown-skinned men with thin moustaches, and they could have been brothers to the .22 caliber victims in Buffalo. In a random selection it would have been extraordinary if two of them had looked alike. None of Gross's five people had noticed the resemblance. Each of them had autopsied only one case. Also, I had the advantage of having seen the upstate victims. It was really an accident that I noticed the faces at all. Wounds are what we examine, not faces. It just happened to hit me.

We felt satisfied with our connection, but it wasn't enough to establish definitely that the Slasher was also the .22 killer. Detectives had found four shell casings (the paper bag had not been foolproof) at the scenes of the shootings, and they had .22 caliber bullets that had been taken out of the victims. They had no gun, but the gun could be traced through the bullets.

Bullets can be identified by their size (.32, .38, etc.) and by the number of lands and grooves they have. While a rifle or handgun is being made, an instrument is fitted into the barrel to rifle it—that is, to make spiral grooves in it. The raised surfaces between the grooves, called lands, put a spin on the bullet (necessary for accuracy). The rifling pattern is imprinted on the bullet as it passes through the barrel when the gun is fired. Every type of gun—every Colt .38, say—has the same number of lands and grooves spiraling in the same direction—left twist or right twist. But there are also microscopic markings made on the bullet as it comes out of the barrel, tiny imperfections that are unique to each gun. Ballistics specialists use them to match up the bullet with the gun it was fired from.

Sam Slade, the homicide detective, took charge of the bullets. He sent them to the FBI crime lab for an analysis of the lands and grooves. The lab reported that the bullets could have been fired from five possible makes of weapons. Four were handguns and one was a rifle. Slade also had shell casings, and the casings bore the imprint of the firing pin, which strikes the back of the bullet. Knowing the imprint, the process of exclusion was easy. Slade got illustrations of firing-pin marks from all five gun manufacturers, and was able to eliminate three of the weapons. The remaining two, a handgun and a rifle, were both made by the Sturm Ruger gun company in Southport, Connecticut. From the company's specifications, the murder weapon had to be a .22 rifle. Slade knew from witnesses that the .22 killer wasn't walking around with a rifle slung over his shoulder. The gun had been hidden in a brown paper bag. That meant the barrel had been sawed off.

In January 1981, a strange story wafted its way to Buffalo from Fort Benning, Georgia. Private Joseph C. Christopher, a white soldier, was arrested for attacking a black soldier with a paring knife. The victim was brown-skinned and youthful and had a thin moustache. Christopher was put into the stockade, where he tried to emasculate himself with a razor blade, after which he was transferred to the base hospital. There he began to unravel and confessed to a nurse that he had killed blacks in Buffalo and New York City, that he "had to" do it. The nurse reported it, and the police immediately connected him with the Buffalo Slasher.

They traced his itinerary, and he was in the right places at the right times. He was the sort of person who kept things, and he still had a bus ticket dated December 19, 1980, from Fort Benning to New York City, where, on December 22, four people were killed with a stiletto. He was on his Christmas furlough. He had continued on to Buffalo, arriving on either Christmas Eve or Christmas Day. While he was there, a black man was stabbed to death at a bus stop, and the next morning another one was killed in the same way in Rochester, eighty miles away. Several other blacks in Buffalo survived stabbing attacks.

Slade got a warrant to search the house in Buffalo where Christopher lived with his mother and sisters. His mother had converted the living room into a shrine, with candles burning under a picture of his dead father. Christopher was born and raised in an Italian neighborhood by a dominant father and a passive mother. His father was a maintenance worker with the Buffalo sanitation department. His mother was a registered nurse. He had three sisters, two of them older than he. He adored his father, Nicholas, an outdoorsman and a hunter, who taught him to shoot. In 1976, when Christopher was fourteen, his father died, and Christopher inherited his gun collection.

In the basement of the house was a workshop. Slade found screwdrivers and hammers and a single bullet that had misfired. The bullet and shell hadn't separated. It matched the firing-pin imprint on the cartridge that Slade had picked up at the scene. Christopher's father also had a hunting lodge forty miles southwest of Buffalo, which Christopher had helped him build. They went there to shoot. On the grass near the house Slade found two spent cartridges. They also matched. The lodge was an armory. He found .22 caliber ammunition, a gun collection, and the sawed-off barrel of a .22 rifle—but not the rifle. The weapon was missing.

Christopher made a videotaped confession to his psychiatrist, admitting to the shootings in Buffalo, the subway slashing in New York, and the murder of the two cabdrivers. A confession alone is not enough—people often come in off the street and confess to all sorts of crimes they may or may not have committed— but Christopher knew things that only the killer could have known. He knew that the second cabdriver had been killed with a screwdriver, and he knew about the saplings. The body of the first cabdriver had been hidden in a wooded area, and saplings had been cut down to cover it. The police hadn't been able to figure out what tool the murderer had used to cut the trunks.

On the videotape, Christopher mentioned in an offhanded way that he had chopped down the saplings with a small hatchet.

Christopher's friends were stunned by his confession. The woman he had once lived with said she couldn't recognize him from the newspaper accounts. "The Joe Christopher I'm reading and hearing about is not the Joe Christopher I knew," she told the *New York Times*.

Other friends, black and white, confirmed that Christopher was singularly ordinary. He had worked as an unarmed guard and as a maintenance man; he liked to hunt and fish (his greatest passion was the outdoors); he was neither angry nor violent nor a racist. In fact, he socialized with blacks and worked with them in the home improvement business. In 1978, two years before the killings began, for no particular reason his life began to fall apart. He broke up with the woman he had been living with and quarreled with his black coworker and friend. He moved back into his mother's house. He fell asleep at his security job and was sacked in 1979. Friends say he started drinking. It was almost as if he had made a conscious decision to shut down his life, or that cycle of it, and go into hibernation. In September 1980, one week before the .22 caliber killings began, he enlisted in the Army. He didn't have to report to Fort Benning until mid-November.

What was his motive? Although Christopher felt compelled to confess, he had no such compulsion to explain himself. He was different from the normal serial killer. He didn't quite fit our preconceived ideas of what he should be. He wasn't killing for fun or for money or even for sex; and he was killing blacks despite the fact that he had black friends. He didn't seem to be killing for hate. He could be one of the hallucinating psychotics, like Son of Sam, the select few who hear God or the devil telling them to kill. He could also be a sexual sadist, a killer for whom the real purpose is a show of physical superiority and aggression. Studies show such people to be outwardly friendly. They have no criminal record before they start their career in murder.

Often there is a conflict with their adult sexuality. Their family and friends are invariably shocked. In these situations, the victim is significant. The victim represents something.

The Army has a theory, a riff on guilt and shame and a sexual conflict that could not be resolved. The Army thinks Christopher is gay. He was friendly with black soldiers, but his relationships had another dimension—he performed fellatio on them in the stockade in return for extra food. He also made a pass at the captain of the stockade. The Army thought he was physically attracted to a particular type (thin, with a moustache), but he knew the men were off limits. So he tried to destroy the thing that was tempting him. By killing them he proved he was macho, like his father. Joining the Army was part of the need to be macho, too, to meet his father's expectations.

The prison psychiatrist, who observed him briefly, thought the truth about Christopher might be simple racism. He had trouble getting along with some of the blacks in prison. But the psychiatrist does not have much information. No effort is made to study the minds of prisoners, to learn what made them killers, and to try to prevent it in the future.

Christopher's trial in Buffalo proceeded without exploring his motives. He was convicted of the three Buffalo .22 caliber shootings, and in New York City he was convicted of the four slashings. Morgenthau apologized to Michael Kelly.

Christopher was not tried for the shooting case in Niagara Falls or for killing the two cabdrivers. Everyone is backing off from those. The method of killing the cabbies was too crazy to risk a trial. If a court should rule that Christopher was mentally incompetent, his other convictions might be questioned and the findings overturned. As things stand, people are safe enough from him. He was put in prison for four murders and can't be considered for parole until 2099. In prison he lives in special housing to protect him from being attacked by blacks. Meanwhile, he was diagnosed as a schizophrenic and is deterioriating.

He is isolated, a loner, and doesn't talk to anyone. He won't even permit blood to be drawn for medical tests.

One other loose end is still dangling. The police never found the sawed-off .22, and it bothered them. Maybe it was at the bottom of the Niagara River, thrown out of the car while Christopher was escaping from the crowd, but maybe it wasn't. Would Joe Christopher throw away his father's gun? More likely he would have hidden it, cherished it. Could he possibly have buried it in his father's grave? It was an intriguing idea. Rumor has it that gravediggers went to the cemetery in the middle of the night and surreptitiously dug up Nicholas Christopher's grave. It is fairly easy to do—you just take off the topsoil with the grass, all in one piece, and then lay it back on the ground when you are finished. The metal detector they brought along picked up a long metal object, and they were elated—they thought they had finally found the gun. But they hadn't; it turned out to be a flower holder.

Richard Kuklinski was a free-lance scammer, a man of many deals, whose business interests included cars, food, and guns. He liked to spray cyanide in people's faces. ". . . there are people . . . all over the country that have died from something . . . that wasn't natural, let's put it that way," he told an undercover agent. An imposing bear of a man, he had the energy and vitality required to keep all his deals going; at the same time, he had taken the precaution of learning about the ME trade. He knew that cold storage was the solution to the alibi problem—if he froze a body for a year or two and then defrosted it, no one could tell the time of death. The police dubbed him the Ice Man (his personality, too, was cold, calculating, icy), but he also kept up with other aspects of forensic medicine, arranging his schemes with our vulnerabilities in mind. He knew that MEs rarely suspect cyanide, and he knew which foods would hide the taste of it. His family was ignorant of his line of work, but they lived a gambler's life—one day they were rolling in money and the next they were broke. His business associates had a way of disappearing after they met with him.

George Malliband of Huntingdon, Pennsylvania, was his first known victim. On January 31, 1980, Malliband left home with $27,000 and met Kuklinski in his office in Emerson, New Jersey. Kuklinski owed him $35,000 from a previous deal, and that, added to the $27,000, made a $62,000 deal for Malliband. Kuklinski was selling him pornographic videos and blank tape at a profit, and Malliband planned to resell them for an even bigger profit.

The day after the meeting, Malliband's brother Donald received several nervous phone calls from him, saying he was afraid Kuklinski was "setting him up." Nobody ever saw or heard from Malliband again. Four days later, he was found in a fifty-five-gallon drum in Jersey City with four gunshot wounds in his chest. His family told the police that while Kuklinski was setting up the deal, he called Malliband fifteen times. On the strength of the phone calls, the police started sniffing around Kuklinski, but they found nothing.

The second scam—a rerun of the videotape deal—was more ambitious. On July 1, 1981, Louis Masgay put together $95,000 in cash, hid it in a secret door panel of his car, and left home to meet Kuklinski in a diner in Little Falls, New Jersey. Masgay was at a pitch of excitement. Kuklinski had been playing him on a string, something he did to perfection. His entire MO was based on the psychology of anticipation. He made numberless phone calls to his mark, luring him on, stirring up his greed and playing on his fear that the deal might fall through. He escalated the amount of cash he needed before the deal could be done. The final twist was withdrawal—not delivering and not delivering until his mark was in a state of high tension. He'd done a particularly fine job on Masgay. In June, the month before this final meeting, Masgay had left his home in Forty-Fort, Pennsylvania, five times to meet Kuklinski, and Kuklinski had stood him up each time. Each time Masgay had been carrying over

$50,000. Now he was frantic to consummate the deal. He had become obsessed with it. He was expecting to make a huge profit, and his family thought that Kuklinski had prevailed on him to bring even more money this last time. On July 1, the day of the meeting, Louis Masgay vanished. That same day his abandoned car was found; the secret panel had been ripped open and the money was gone.

Two years later, in September 1983, Masgay's body was found in Rockland County, New York, wrapped in plastic bags and wearing the same clothes he had worn on the day of his disappearance. Like his predecessor, he had been shot, but he had only just begun to decay. He looked fresh, as if he had died the day before. When the ME did the autopsy, he noticed ice in the tissues. Kuklinski had miscalculated slightly—the plastic wrapping had kept the cold in, and the body had been found a little early, before the ice had melted completely. Masgay was identified from his fingerprints, after which the police were able to connect him with Kuklinski through the toll phone calls. They later found a witness (a convicted murderer) who had worked for Kuklinski in his rented warehouse in North Bergen. The warehouse contained an industrial freezer, an abandoned well, and other amenities. The witness had had occasion to go into the freezer and had seen Masgay hanging there, but had decided not to mention it to anyone lest he end up keeping Masgay company.

Kuklinski was aware by now that the police were interested in his affairs and became more cautious. For his next victim he assumed the name of Charlie Brown. On April 29, 1982, Paul Hoffman, a pharmacist, went to meet him with $25,000. This time the bait was a hijacked shipment of Tagamet. Tagamet is a prescription drug to ease the pain of ulcers. It was the most frequently prescribed drug in the country. The going rate was $36.00 for 100 tablets. Hoffman was going to buy it for $9. Like Masgay, Hoffman became obsessed. His wife and son and partner remember him getting calls and then, after talking about the deal, becoming irritable and frustrated, fearful that it might not go through. On the few occasions when they picked up the phone, a man named Charlie Brown was on the other end. The police traced the toll calls to Kuklinski. In five months, Kuklinski had called Hoffman forty-five times. After April 29, the day they were to meet, the calls stopped.

Hoffman and his station wagon both disappeared. A year later, the car was found in Kuklinski's rented warehouse, where he stored and moved cars for his auto-theft business. Hoffman's body was never recovered, but the police think they have a good idea of what happened to it. The people who rented the warehouse after Kuklinski left noticed a foul odor coming from the abandoned well, which had been capped with cement. The police went down, but all they saw were some plastic bags and other debris. The well narrowed and fed into an underground stream, and they could follow it no farther.

Bits and pieces of evidence were gradually piling up against Kuklinski. There wasn't nearly enough to arrest him, but two of his associates, Daniel Deppner and Gary Smith, hadn't been so clever at covering their tracks. On December 17, 1982, the police issued a warrant for Deppner, charging him with stealing cars. Smith's warrant was out already, charging him with stealing checks and cashing them. They searched Smith's house, where both men lived, but the two of them had already run to Kuklinski, who hid them in various New Jersey motels—the York, the Liberty, the Skyview—and fed them.

It wasn't long before Kuklinski began to worry about their stability. He couldn't hide them indefinitely, and Smith, in particular, had a weak personality. If he were caught he would not be tough enough to withstand the pressures; he would make a deal to save his own neck and be a witness against Kuklinski. With Deppner assisting, Kuklinski killed Smith in Room 31 of the York Motel. It was a two-step operation—first the cyanide and then the lamp cord. Kuklinski, who was supplying the food, cooked meals at home and brought them to the motel in a Teflon pan. Smith liked hamburgers, which made things a little difficult—as Kuklinski later observed, you can't sprinkle cyanide on hamburgers; nobody would eat them with white stuff all over them. So he had to mix the cyanide into the ketchup. The purpose of the cyanide was mainly to knock Smith out (people have been known to survive doses of cyanide), preparatory to the main event—strangulation. No adult will permit himself to be strangled without putting up a fight, and Kuklinski was not interested in a physical struggle.

They put Smith's body under the bed, which had a wooden platform frame and box springs. The York Motel, which is just across the Lincoln Tunnel from Manhattan, had a high turnover rate. In December the rooms were warm; the heat was turned up to 80 degrees. Beneath the bed in the closed space it was about 100 degrees. Smith stayed under there for four days, during which time the room was rented more than a dozen times. The maid, who changed the sheets occasionally, complained about the smell, but the spring was on top of the body and she couldn't see under the bed. Smith was finally found on December 27.

The Bergen County ME who did the autopsy couldn't find the cause of death, but Dr. Geetha Natarajan, New Jersey assistant ME, saw a ligature mark around the neck, a furrow about as thin as an electrical wire from a lamp. She also observed that the beans in the stomach were charred at one end, and concluded that they were probably homemade. What restaurant would serve burned beans? Kuklinski had been right. No one looked for cyanide. There was no reason to.

During their ten-day motel shuffle, Smith and Deppner had called their wives frequently. Before his death, Smith told his wife, Veronica, he was afraid for his life. Deppner told his, Barbara, everything—that the three of them stole cars and transported them out of the state and ran chop shops. He called her before and after killing Smith, and told her how it was done, and that he thought he, too, was becoming dispensable. Barbara tried to save him: she told the police the story and asked them to protect him. In January 1983, the month after Smith's body was found, the police started looking for him. They wanted him for burglary, car theft, and stealing car parts. He was still broke and dependent on Kuklinski, who was still moving him from one motel to another under assumed names and feeding him. Kuklinski decided he had to go.

In May, a man riding a bicycle on Clinton Road in West Milford, New Jersey, near Passaic, saw a large bird—he thought it was a turkey buzzard—lift off and fly away. He went closer and saw a plastic garbage bag with a human head sticking out of it. It had a bushy, reddish Fu Manchu moustache and was missing four front teeth. The left arm was also sticking out. The body was inside two green garbage bags that were taped together in the middle. The police found motel receipts and private phone numbers in a pocket. The site was about three and a half miles from the Blazing Bucks Ranch, a property Kuklinski had an interest in. At some time in February, Kuklinski had asked his daughter's live-in fiancé, Richard Patterson, to help him get rid of something in the woods. Patterson was agreeable, but after catching a glimpse of what he was getting rid of he decided this was not the sort of family he wanted to marry into and relocated to Florida.

Dr. Natarajan did the autopsy. She found processed meat—hot dogs or Spam—and the same curiously burned beans in Deppner's stomach as she had found in Gary Smith's. She also saw a ligature mark on the neck and thought the cause was strangulation. From the way the body was discovered and from the lack of any other cause—no gunshot wound, no stab wound, no blunt force, no heart disease, no brain damage—it had to be murder. Her conclusion was based partly on instinct and partly on experience—the way we all operate. But her office didn't think this exclusionary process was strong enough to call the death a murder and thought the ligature mark could be an artifact of decomposition. Natarajan was certain enough of the ligature mark to call the manner of death a homicide, but signed it out as "cause undetermined."

At this point the police had a stack of murders and a chief suspect but no hard evidence and no witnesses. Someone had to go undercover to smoke out Kuklinski. Kuklinski had been dealing in weapons, promising buyers guns for cash, and this opened the door to the Feds. The Bureau of Alcohol, Tobacco, and Firearms wired one of its agents, Dominick Polifrone, and sent him in. Polifrone started hanging around one of Kuklinski's favorite bars. They met in September 1986, and in the course of establishing his credentials, Polifrone had to get up and punch someone.

Most of their conversations took place at the Vincent Lombardi truck stop on the New Jersey Turnpike, known as a favorite hangout for dealmakers trying to score. Polifrone's fellow agents sat in a car nearby, recording. Kuklinski kept wanting to talk in the bathroom, and Polifrone was never sure if he was on to him. He always refused. His fellow agents couldn't prevent Kuklinski from killing him in a bathroom.

It took a few weeks for the deal to take shape. They sparred back and forth, each offering a challenge, each trying to fool the other. Kuklinski was interested in cocaine. Polifrone said he could handle that—he could sell Kuklinski a kilo for $31,000. He would get it from a "rich kid." (The rich kid was really Paul Smith, another agent.) To make sure that Kuklinski knew he was a cold-blooded businessman, Polifrone suggested that they kill the kid and split the money—Polifrone would set him up and Kuklinski would waste him. Polifrone said he was looking for guns, "heavy steel." That was no problem for Kuklinski. He had a supplier who could get machine guns, grenades, silencers, plastique, everything—and all of it Grade A NATO stuff.

Kuklinski discoursed on the advantages of cyanide—"It's quiet, it's not messy, it's not noisy . . . there's even a spray mist around . . . you spray it in somebody's face and they go to sleep. . . ." He was a throwback to the old Murder, Inc., crowd.

He described a test murder he had committed on the street, just walking along in a crowd with a handkerchief over his nose and spraying a man. The man collapsed and died, and everyone thought he'd had a heart attack. "The best effect is to get 'em in the nose, they get it in the nose, and they inhale it," he said. But he wasn't married to this method—if Polifrone wanted to give him a contract, he could do it with lead, steel, anything.

Kuklinski also boasted that he had used cyanide to kill other people, and had outwitted the police—they had been watching him since 1980 and couldn't pin anything on him. He'd even frozen a corpse to confuse the time of death. He told Polifrone how he put someone in a fifty-five-gallon drum (no names were mentioned), and described his one-two method of killing with cyanide and strangulation. Polifrone knew that Kuklinski wouldn't be telling him all these secrets unless he was planning to kill him. The only question was when.

The deal finally began to come together in October at a truck stop in Ridgefield, New Jersey. Kuklinski sold Polifrone a first-quality handgun with a silencer for $1,100 (a sample of future attractions) and agreed to kill the "rich kid." He would do it with poison. (". . . why be messy?" he said on the tapes. "You do it nice and calm.") But Polifrone would have to supply the cyanide—ever since his regular supplier, Paul Hoffman the pharmacist, had disappeared down the well, his cache had dwindled. After this act of bonding, they would do the arms deal. Polifrone would deliver the money, and instead of getting guns, he would get killed.

They worked with beepers. Kuklinski beeped Polifrone to ask if he had "the big package" (cocaine) and "the little package" (cyanide) yet—he was ready to buy. Polifrone wasn't ready to sell yet—there had been an incident of tampering with Lipton Soup in a grocery store, and things were tight. Would Polifrone like to meet Kuklinski's armaments friend? No, Polifrone definitely would not. (It would be two against one, and prearranged meetings were dangerous. Other things could be prearranged, too.)

On December 17 they met at the Lombardi truck stop. Polifrone brought three scrambled egg sandwiches and a jar of quinine—a cyanide look-alike—to put on them. They would meet the "rich kid" at a motel (Polifrone had already pointed him out to Kuklinski) and socialize a little. After lunch they would take his cocaine and strangle him. The strangling was just to make sure. For all his cavalier attitude about cyanide, Kuklinski did not seem to know the exact amount needed to kill—less than 200 milligrams, or the contents of one capsule.

Kuklinski took the sandwiches and went home, promising to return with a van, a drum and sealer, gloves, and whatever else was necessary to dispose of the body. But the police were too nervous to let it go any further. They weren't sure what surprises he might be cooking up—for all they knew, a couple of men with guns would suddenly appear and blow Polifrone away. They gave Kuklinski ten minutes to doctor the rich kid's sandwich—and maybe Polifrone's, too—and then arrested him, charging him with five murders. His wife was in the car and a handgun was under the seat. They charged her with possession. (They never found out if Kuklinski had doctored one sandwich or two. The toxicologist at the New Jersey crime lab who tested the sandwiches put all three together and mashed them up. He found quinine throughout.)

The police had an impressive case. All along they had been generating leads and witnesses. They had a witness who saw Hoffman's car in the warehouse and another who saw Masgay's body in the freezer; they had the ex-fiancé in Florida and Polifrone's tapes and the quinine sandwiches; they had Barbara Deppner's recital of her husband's confession. But it was all circumstantial, without any hard medical evidence. No cyanide had been found in the bodies. The defense took the tack that Kuklinski had invented the stories on the tapes—he hadn't really poisoned anybody; it was all just "puffery," macho brag-

ging. There was also a problem with Deppner's cause of death.
Natarajan had picked up the ligature marks on his neck and
called it murder. She hadn't considered cyanide. The body was
too decomposed to find it, and if you have one cause you don't
look for another. With no cyanide and a death by cause undetermined, the case against Kuklinski was weakened further. Had
Kuklinski been lying? The state attorney general asked me to
take a separate look before the trial to see if his taped confessions
squared with the evidence.

Listening to the tapes, I thought Kuklinski knew too much.
He couldn't have made up the stories if he hadn't done just what
he said. His knowledge was too detailed. The irony of it was that
if he hadn't strangled Smith and Deppner, no one would have
thought of murder. Smith could have been left on top of the bed
and been called a drug overdose or a suicide in a motel.

The defense was saying that no cyanide was found in the bodies, but the absence of cyanide didn't mean they weren't given
it. After a few days you can't find cyanide in a body. That's one
of the reasons it's such a good murder weapon. It breaks apart
into carbon and nitrogen. The distinctive odor of bitter almonds
is only discernible on a fresh body; it is lost as the body decomposes. But the cyanide didn't become entirely invisible—it
showed up in the lividity. With the advantage of knowing the
history of the case and seeing the pictures, I realized that Smith
and Deppner both had patches of skin with the peculiar shade
of red that comes from cyanide poisoning. They both had the
lividity, and they both had marks around their neck. This was
the proof, and it was entirely consistent with Kuklinski's stories
to Polifrone. He had been telling the truth.

When I took the witness stand for the prosecution, some of
my cyanide testimony was on the order of a double negative.
The lividity proved that it *could* have been cyanide, I said (without the toxicology I couldn't be more definite), so you couldn't
say Kuklinski was not telling the truth. It was convoluted, but
the jury agreed with it. They found him guilty of murdering

Smith and Deppner, and he was sentenced to life. The minimum time he has to serve is sixty years.

Kuklinski wasn't tried for the other three killings. A second trial would have cost the state too much money, time, and effort. Instead, the DA used it as a bargaining chip. He wanted Kuklinski to plead guilty to the deaths of Malliband, Masgay, and Hoffman so he could close the cases. It looks sloppy and incompetent to have a lot of unsolved murders clogging up the books. Kuklinski agreed (including the missing body of Paul Hoffman). In return, the DA promised to leave his wife and children alone. His wife had been charged with illegal possession of a gun (it was in the car when the police caught him), and his son had been caught with marijuana. The charges were dropped.

Kuklinski still has one last secret. No one knows where he disposed of Hoffman's body. At first he told the police he would show them, but then he backed off. You never know when you might need a card to deal with. He still has something they want.

9

ALMOST PERFECT

WITHOUT A TRACE

A PERFECT MURDER is like a perfect scam—only the killer, the mastermind, knows how it was done or even that it happened. There is no suspicion and no investigation. For us, "perfect" murders are those that are difficult to prove from an autopsy. They are deaths for which we can find either the cause or the manner but not both. In smothering (or burking) which leaves no sign, we cannot be certain it happened. In drowning or falling from a height, we cannot determine whether it was an accident, suicide, or homicide. Often, we have to rely on clues at the scene not present in the autopsy room.

At a defenestration there are two scenes, the one upstairs and the one downstairs. Downstairs is the mute body. Upstairs are all the things it can no longer tell us—a suicide note, the signs of a struggle, one window that looks cleaner than the others. At one scene I found a bloody hat with a long cut across the top. I pieced together the dead man's skull bones, and there on his crown was the impact of a meat cleaver. His roommate confessed. They had fought over drugs; the roommate had killed him and thrown him out the window. The apartment was nine stories high, and he thought the injury would be hidden in the general mess of the impact. It could have been. But he wasn't very lucky, and he forgot something. He forgot to get rid of the hat.

Drowning deaths also need interpretation. On the surface it seems obvious—you drown because you are inhaling water instead of oxygen. But the lungs also fill with fluid in heart failure and in drug deaths. When the heart stops pumping, water accumulates in the lungs and froth forms in the mouth. As we saw with John Belushi, the same thing happens in a heroin overdose—fluid seeps out of the blood and works its way to the nose and mouth. We have to look for other clues. Generally speaking, if we find what looks like a drowning on a rooftop, we know it's drugs. If we find it in an elderly person at home with digitalis pills, it's heart failure.

The air-conditioning was turned up high and the house was freezing when the nude body of Paul Fried was discovered on July 23, 1976. Fried, a prominent Philadelphia gynecologist, was lying face down on the bedroom floor of his house near Rittenhouse Square. His nose was bloodied and there was a blood-stained pillow over his head. He was sixty-one years old. His wife, Catherine, was in her thirties, and they had been married for only a year. She had been worried that something like this might happen, she told the police. Her husband was an alcohol and barbiturate addict, and he had become suicidal. That very morning she had gone to Dr. Robert Brotman, a psychiatrist, to talk about ways to help him. She had been calling the house and couldn't get an answer and, apparently nervous about what she might find, had asked the psychiatrist and Ruth Kennedy, her business partner, to come with her.

The police found a note on the bedside table. The handwriting was shaky and a little difficult to read. It looked like a name—Flower, or maybe Glower?—and a phone number. From the number they figured out the name—Glauser. Glauser was Paul Fried's accountant. And under the name was the word "pills." They interpreted it as being a suicide note. Suicide notes are seldom neat, literate essays. If there's a dead body and the scene looks innocent, the police interpret the death as a suicide. There's always a subjective evaluation of what happened, an instant perception of the scene. If it looks natural or accidental, you make the rest of your judgments in that light. If you believe the distraught spouse, you give him or her more credibility.

It took ten years to establish that Paul Fried had been murdered.

On the strength of Catherine Fried's story, Dr. Halbert Fillinger, the assistant ME, did only a limited examination. He was usually more careful, but he was persuaded it was a sleeping-pill overdose, just as Catherine had said, and he sent the stomach contents to a lab for chemical analysis. Even before the results came back, he issued the death certificate—drug overdose, suicide.

Calling the death a suicide triggered alarm bells for Fried's three daughters from his first marriage. They would have accepted a natural death, but suicide was unthinkable. Carlie, the eldest, couldn't believe such a thing of her father. He would never commit suicide. His father had killed himself, and Paul regarded it as a contemptible weakness, a disgraceful act. Furious, the daughters went to Fillinger's superior, the chief ME of Philadelphia, Marvin E. Aronson. The family can always appeal the cause of death, and Aronson could have been expected to sit down and go over the records with them. They wanted a full autopsy. But Catherine, who knew Aronson socially, had asked him to hasten the removal of the body from the ME's office to a funeral home. He did, and she had it embalmed, even though she was planning to cremate it. The children got an injunction to halt the cremation and hired Milton Helpern to do a second autopsy, over Catherine's objections. (After he finished, Catherine's fit of urgency passed. She left the body unclaimed in the ME's office for over six months before cremating it.)

Helpern, who had only a few more months left to live, had become a little fuzzy, but he performed with brio. He described pinpoint hemorrhages in the eyes and bruises on the neck, but did not think they were particularly significant. In a fifteen-page report, he discoursed eloquently on the human body as "a museum" of pathological exhibits—he found hardening of the arteries of the heart and kidneys, benign tumors in the adrenal glands, lumps in the thyroid—but none of these, except for the hardening of the heart arteries, was life-threatening. He waxed poetic about the aging of the body, the changes and abnormalities in all of us as we grow older. And he finally decided that Paul Fried had died of natural causes. Aronson changed the death certificate to "cause undetermined," and the children felt much better. The stigma was gone. The case was finished.

About a year later, Jerald Sklar, a good-looking, intelligent former teacher who had been working in Catherine Fried's employment agency, contacted the Philadelphia office of the FBI and offered to make a deal. He would tell the FBI about three murders it didn't know about, and in exchange, he wanted a new career. He wanted to get into the Federal Witness Protection Program; he wanted a guaranteed income, and he wanted the FBI to get him into Harvard Law School. (If he had known a little more about the law, he might have tried to make a different kind of bargain. He thought he had immunity.)

Sklar confessed to hiring a killer to get rid of two business associates of his friend Michael Melvin Selkow, an underworld hustler and con man. Selkow owed them a lot of money and was not prepared to pay it. The third murder he knew about was Paul Fried's. He knew that Catherine had sat on his face and smothered him. She had told him about it. She had put a pillow over her husband's face and braced it with her knees and held down his wrists with her hands. She enjoyed it so much, she told Sklar, that she had the best orgasm she ever had in her life.

Catherine had never planned to kill her husband. All along she had been trying to get someone else to do it for her—first Selkow and then Sklar. Sklar had introduced her to Selkow in June 1975, a month before her marriage, telling her he had Mafia connections. Intrigued, she began an affair with him and gave him $2,000. She was planning to spend the weekend of the Fourth of July with him, but at the last minute she stood him up and flew off to Las Vegas to marry Fried. It was the third marriage for each. The day before the wedding, they signed individual prenuptial agreements, each renouncing all rights to the other's property. (As Paul's wife, Catherine would legally have been entitled to one third of his $450,000 estate.) On her return, she phoned Selkow to tell him the marriage was only a temporary interruption of their affair. She didn't plan to "live out the marriage," and in fact it had not been consummated. She and Paul were going to keep it a secret and maintain separate residences.

Two weeks after the wedding, Catherine showed Selkow some bruises which she said Paul had inflicted on her, and asked him to murder Paul. Selkow declined, but offered to bring over a hit man from Italy for the sum of $25,000. Catherine gave him a down payment of over $9,000.

On his side, Paul had not been idle. He told his lawyer that Catherine refused to sleep with him, and a few weeks after the wedding he had divorce papers served on her.

Weeks went by, and the arrival of Selkow's hit man kept being delayed. Catherine vacillated. It occurred to her that Selkow was ripping her off, and she decided to cancel the hit man. Selkow told her the cancellation fee was an additional $6,000. She sent him a letter ending their affair. Belying her tough, Lady Macbeth exterior, she wrote, "I'm grateful for the attention you gave me and am pleased to have paid for it. I felt so lonely and alone that I would have—that I would gladly have paid you a million dollars for half the attention you gave me. . . . I know that I'm not good company, nor a good screw, and all I can say is thank you." She thought the $9,000 down payment would cover the $6,000 cancellation fee.

Catherine and Paul reconciled. She and her two daughters from a previous marriage lived with him in his townhouse, trying to make a go of it. It was an uneasy truce, frequently shattered by bitter arguments. They fought over money constantly, verbally and physically. Neighbors said they were both black and blue, a pair of battered spouses.

Early in 1976, Catherine and her daughters moved a few blocks away to an apartment on the twenty-sixth floor of a luxury high rise, but she and Paul remained on their roller coaster. A few months later she found him injured at home, his face bruised, his speech slurred. In the hospital he confessed to his doctor that he had been drinking and doing drugs, and later he tried to destroy the hospital records. Two months before the murder he fell down the stairs of his townhouse and broke a small bone in the back of his neck. This time he stayed in the hospital to dry out. While he was resting and recuperating, Catherine and Selkow, a man she couldn't stay away from, broke into Paul's safe and stole $6,000 (no connection to the $6,000 cancellation fee; it just happened to be there) and her original prenuptial agreement. They left his. When Paul got out of the hospital, she cared for him in her apartment.

By now it was June 1976. The year of marriage had been a year of violence and disappointment. Catherine had had enough, and she tried again to have her husband murdered. This time she went to Jerald Sklar, who was working in her employment agency. In the presence of Ruth Kennedy, her partner, she begged him repeatedly to help her. It was really very simple. All she wanted him to do was push Paul off her twenty-sixth-floor balcony. The police would think it was a drunken accident. She would let Sklar take some of the art in Paul's collection—it was valuable stuff—in partial payment. Sklar didn't find the offer tempting enough, and she sweetened the pot with $50,000. He turned her down. She didn't have $50,000, he said. She didn't have it right now, she told him, but she would get it from the estate after he did the deed.

Things became critical in July. Neighbors called the police to break up a fight. Catherine, screaming that she would kill Paul, had to be physically restrained. On another occasion, after Catherine had gone to work, Paul telephoned his nurse. Catherine had been hitting him in his neck fracture, and he wanted to go back to his own house. Soon thereafter, the doorman called Catherine at work—Paul was moving out with his suitcase and some appliances, trying to load his car. Catherine grabbed Sklar and ran home through the streets, shoving people out of her way as she ran. How dare he take things out of her house! She confronted Paul on the sidewalk, where they had another of their hitting and shoving matches. Again the police arrived, and again she threatened to kill Paul, who now had less than forty-eight hours to live.

Back at the office, Catherine threw a set of keys at Sklar and harangued him all afternoon to kill her husband. She could talk of nothing else. Sklar continued to refuse, but prudently kept the keys long enough to have duplicates made. (On the weekend after Paul's death, when the house was empty, he and Selkow used the keys and cleaned out the place. Catherine was enraged. They had received payment for a job they hadn't done.)

The next day Catherine finally realized that nobody was going to do it for her, and began constructing a smoke screen. She spent most of the day on the telephone with doctors and lawyers, seeking advice about her poor alcoholic, drug-ridden doctor husband—how to help him, places to dry him out, ways to handle him. She called Dr. Robert Brotman, chief psychiatrist at the outpatient clinic at Jefferson Hospital (the same hospital where Paul taught), asking to have Paul committed involuntarily—he had hit her, he was refusing to seek treatment for his drug and alcohol habits, and he was suicidal. Brotman, who had never seen either of them professionally, agreed to talk to her in his office at 9:00 the following morning. More reluctantly, he agreed to interview her husband at home.

That evening she visited Paul to feed him. She poured a big glass of liquor for him and brought it up to his bedroom. She made a last-ditch effort to enlist Sklar's services, but he refused. (Those who later prosecuted the case were not entirely convinced of his innocence, but there was no proof.) Later in the evening she returned, bringing a hamburger for Paul's dinner, and invited a neighbor to come in with her. Still later, at about 2:30 A.M., she returned once more, this time silently and alone. She had created something of a cover for herself with the first two visits—Paul was alive both times when she left. The third time she suffocated him. Before leaving she rolled the body onto the floor and took the phone off the hook. She also had the presence of mind to remove $7,000 from the safe.

At 9:00 the next morning, Catherine kept her appointment with Brotman. From his office she called Paul, but the line was continuously busy. She was fearful that something had happened, and Brotman agreed to go back with her. He later said it was an odd request, and it took him a long time to realize he had been set up. Brotman pronounced Paul dead. The police were not suspicious—there was no forced entry, no sign of trauma—and Catherine explained about Paul's history of drug and alcohol abuse. He'd been popping pills all week, she said, and he was suicidal.

All of this was Sklar's story. Catherine had confessed to him, not to the police. If Ruth Kennedy hadn't been in the office to hear some of it, no one would have paid any attention. Sklar's word alone would have been almost worthless. Until his bombshell, the possibility of murder hadn't occurred to anyone. It is unusual for a woman to strangle or suffocate a man—or for a man to strangle another man, for that matter. Almost all strangulations between the sexes are men strangling women. Catherine was five feet three and weighed 105 pounds; Paul was five feet seven and weighed 151 pounds, but he was wearing a neck brace, which would have limited his ability to move his head, and he was woozy from painkillers, which slowed down his reactions. Physically, it was entirely feasible. But Clifford Hanes, the Philadelphia DA, wasn't sure he really had a case to prosecute. He was having trouble reconciling the two different autopsy findings—first suicide and then natural causes—with the newest cause, suffocation by pillow. He asked me for my opinion.

The body had been cremated, so I reviewed the records and photographs. And I saw that Milton Helpern's report had unwittingly described suffocation—pinpoint hemorrhages in the eyes and bruises on the face and neck. Pinpoint hemorrhages typically appear with manual strangulation, but they are not necessarily always there with smothering. They can develop naturally if the body is lying face down, as Paul Fried's was. Essentially, they come from burst capillaries, and figuring out how the capillaries burst is a matter of context. It's judgment and interpretation and your sense of the scene, the physical condition of the rest of the body. It was suspicious to me that the body was found on the floor. Natural deaths tend to take place in bed. Even with a heart attack or a stroke, most people manage to get to a bed before collapsing. The toxicology report, which came back from the lab after the first death certificate had been signed (the one that gave alcohol and drug overdose as the cause), and which no one seems to have looked at, showed no alcohol and a very low level of barbiturates. Without barbiturates, there was no suicide. The report contradicted the findings of both suicide and accidental overdose. Paul had a bad heart, but Helpern's slides and photographs showed no evidence of a heart attack. However, given Paul's heart condition, he would suffocate faster if he was deprived of oxygen. Considering all these things, Sklar's tale began to assume a great deal of credibility, mainly because it was consistent with the autopsy findings. A confession that reflects the autopsy findings is highly believable. People who just make things up can't explain the medical evidence.

The prosecutor agreed with me, but he chose that moment to move into private practice. The assistant DA, Hal Rosenberg, inherited the case, along with his assistant, James Jordan. They were perfect contrasts. Rosenberg was emotional and enthusiastic; Jordan was cool and reticent. (Rosenberg later became one of the lead counsels against Johns-Manville in the asbestos cases; Jordan has since become a partner in a prestigious law firm.) Both of them were reasonably certain that Catherine was guilty, but they lacked hard cold evidence—a witness who actually saw the suffocation, say. The confession didn't even come from her—it was indirect, secondhand, something she allegedly said to someone else. They were relying on the statement of Sklar, a professional liar who had already confessed to two murders. The only real corroboration was the autopsy finding, and even that was not very strong. I couldn't say with absolute certainty that the cause of death was suffocation. I couldn't even say that a crime had been committed. The fact of the crime—the corpus delicti—has to be established by evidence other than the confession. Neither the confession nor other incriminating statements could be admitted into evidence until the corpus delicti had been proved. The judge would not let me take into account anything except the physical evidence of Paul's body. I couldn't discuss the scene or the possibilities. The only thing I could say was "consistent with suffocation."

Among Catherine's chief defense witnesses were the two medical examiners who had signed the conflicting death certificates—Halbert Fillinger and Marvin Aronson, now working privately. Few lawyers are prepared to examine MEs properly. They don't know the right questions to ask. And the ME, if he chooses, can hide behind medical terms and peripheral issues, stonewall, and intone gibberish, with no one the wiser. Rosenberg and Jordan did their homework. They laced into Fillinger and Aronson and demolished both causes of death—suicide and natural—and then I offered the signs of suffocation, subtle but visible. The jury came back with a verdict of guilty, but it doubtless had other reasons in addition to the medical ones for doing so. Jordan thought the heavy and brutish appearance of Michael Selkow, who testified that he and Catherine were lovers, was extremely helpful to the prosecution. The jury, he thought, wondered what kind of a woman would sleep with a man like that. It cast her in a bad light.

Catherine appealed and won on the ground that there was insufficient evidence of the corpus delicti. The case was sent back for a new trial. This time a different judge allowed me to take into account the circumstances and history, and I was able to say that Paul Fried had very likely been suffocated. Suffocation is never definite. Again, the jury found Catherine guilty, and again she appealed.

Jerald Sklar, who wanted to go to Harvard, was convicted of the two murders he said he'd hired a killer to commit for Selkow and is serving two life sentences. The jury thought he did them himself. Selkow fared rather better. After being caught in a drug deal, he allowed himself to be wired and used as a witness against his former associates. Catherine's passionate affair with him is on hold while she is in jail.

Poisons and drugs are also invisible killers, but they have one great disadvantage—the person administering them has to be physically close to the victim, which immediately puts him at the top of the list of suspects. Nevertheless, doctors gravitate toward them. They are easy to get, and a well-chosen poison quickly breaks down into its elements and may never be found at all. Drs. Carl Coppolino and Mario Jascalevich may well have counted on that when each of them embarked on his misadventure.

Carl Coppolino, a slim, dark, and attractive anesthesiologist at Riverview Hospital in Red Bank, New Jersey, was a successful womanizer who lived with his wife, Carmela, in nearby Middletown. Carmela, also a doctor, worked at Hoffman-LaRoche Pharmaceutical Company. While in his early thirties, Carl developed a heart condition and had to spend much of his time at home, living on compensation from his disability policy. (It was later discovered that he was secretly taking digitalis. Digitalis causes abnormal lines in electrocardiograms which are easily mistaken for heart disease.) While his wife was out working, Carl passed the time by having an affair with a neighbor, Marjorie Farber. Her husband, William E. Farber, was a fifty-four-year-old insurance executive and retired Army colonel. It was a hypnotic affair. Carl mesmerized Marge out of smoking, and she felt herself to be living entirely under his spell, her will bonded to his. With the knowledge of Carmela, who was a trusting soul, they took trips to Florida, Atlantic City, and San Juan. As Marge later testified, one day Carl said, "That man has got to go," meaning her husband. An anesthesiologist, Carl turned to an anesthetic for his weapon, and ordered a number of vials of succinylcholine from a drug company. (Later, when he was asked what he needed them for, he explained that he was doing cat experiments, but he hadn't kept any records of them.)

Succinylcholine is artificial curare. It is used during operations the way Pavulon is—to relax skeletal muscles. This makes it possible to administer lighter doses of other more dangerous anesthetics. A continuous IV drip of succinylcholine causes muscle paralysis, but a single injection doesn't last very long—the drug breaks down in the body without causing harm. Carl tried to get Marge to inject her husband, but she couldn't quite manage it, and he finally had to do it himself. The colonel hung onto life stubbornly, not believing that his time had come. Carl was forced to resort to smothering him with a pillow, but the colonel still refused to succumb. In the struggle, Carl strangled the colonel with his bare hands, although Marge did not see it. Later, one of her daughters came home and noticed that "Daddy looks funny." As instructed by Carl, Marge called Carmela, who signed the death certificate, giving coronary thrombosis as the cause. Nobody thought that anything was amiss.

Two years later, in 1965, Carl and Carmela and their two chil-

dren moved to Sarasota, Florida. Marge already had property
there, and she decided to move down and live on it. Carl asked
Carmela for a divorce, but she refused. A few months later, in
August, Carmela, who was insured, was found dead. Carl called
an acquaintance, Dr. Juliette Karow, who lived nearby. He was
in a peculiar position, he said, and there were niceties to be observed. His wife had just died of a heart attack, but he had
qualms about signing the death certificate—it just wouldn't look
right—and could Dr. Karow sign it? Dr. Karow signed Carmela
out as a coronary occlusion. Carmela's father, Carmelo Musetto,
who was also a doctor, was astounded to learn that his thirty-
two-year-old daughter had had a bad heart. How do you know?
he asked Carl, and Carl explained that it had showed up in Carmela's autopsy. He shipped the body back to New Jersey to be
buried.

Until now, Carl had been doing very well. He'd gotten rid
of two superfluous people with no suspicion attaching to him;
and he was making a living, if an unconventional one. At this
point he stumbled. One and a half months after Carmela's death
he remarried, but not to his longtime lover, Marge. Marge was
getting on. She was already past fifty, and he was only thirty-
four. He married Mary Gibson, thirty-eight, whom he had met
in Sarasota playing bridge. Marge, whose patience had gone un-
rewarded all this time, was devastated and started spreading the
story. First she told Dr. Karow, then Dr. Karow's priest, who
advised her to inform the FBI. Instead, she went to the sheriff
and said that Carl had probably killed his wife the same way
he had killed her husband, by injecting Carmela with succinylcholine. The sheriff called Vincent Keuper, the Monmouth
County, New Jersey, prosecutor. Keuper was at a loss. He called
G. Malcolm B. Gilman, the ME for Monmouth County. Gilman, who traced his ancestors back to the *Mayflower,* had a
strong sense of history but a shaky concept of his job. He didn't
know what to do, either. They called Helpern in New York. He
would know what to do.

Meanwhile, Dr. Carmelo Musetto, who had moved to Sarasota to be with his grandchildren, went to the Florida prosecutor. Musetto had actually known since the funeral that there had been no autopsy and Carl had lied to him. The New Jersey undertaker who had buried Carmela had told him. He had been afraid to say anything for fear that Carl would prevent him from seeing his grandchildren. He later testified, "I was lost. I was a lost man," to explain his curious silence.

With two people raising the alarm (the word of Marge, a jilted woman, was not enough), the New Jersey DA decided to investigate. Helpern exhumed Carmela first. She had been dead only four months. The colonel had been dead two and a half years, and exhuming such long-buried bodies was rarely done then. I assisted Helpern in our Decomposed Room, which is about twenty by twenty-five feet and is specially ventilated. In the center are two steel autopsy tables with running water. Around the walls are glass cabinets with jars containing body parts; there are electric saws and other instruments. G. Malcolm B. Gilman sat on a stool and watched. Because of Marge's accusation, we looked for injections first. Without her, we might never have found anything. We went over Carmela with a magnifying lens. Mold covered her face (usually found in exhumed bodies) and preserved the skin underneath by absorbing moisture. The most common sites of injections are the fleshy parts of the body—the shoulders, arms, thighs, and buttocks. We found a puncture wound in the left buttock. It looked like a little anthill. Helpern cut through it with a scalpel and saw a thin hemorrhagic needle mark, a puncture that went down through the skin. Marge's jilted-woman ravings achieved instant credibility. There was no reason for the injection. And Carmela had no heart disease. The mark of the injection was clear, but it was unlikely that succinylcholine had worked any better on Carmela than it had on the colonel. The prosecutor theorized that Carmela had been lying on her stomach, possibly asleep, and Carl had caught her unawares. He sat on her, which prevented her from moving and interfered with her breathing. The injection paralyzed her, making it easy for Carl to smother her with a pillow.

Colonel Farber was in Arlington Cemetery. It was wet inside his coffin, and his uniform looked better than he did. The tissues in front of his neck had deteriorated, but we found fractures of his right and left cricoid cartilages, just under the Adam's apple—he had a fractured larynx, which in this instance meant manual strangulation. His heart was well preserved and showed no evidence of a heart attack.

Carl was tried twice, once for the colonel's death in New Jersey and once for his wife's in Florida. The colonel went first. The case for Carl's having killed him was stronger—manual strangulation and an eyewitness, Marge. Both times F. Lee Bailey defended him. Bailey was at his peak, dramatic and exciting, drawing publicity like a magnet. He had a tremendous presence, and commanded the courtroom. His defense was that Colonel Farber had died of heart disease. He had not been murdered and therefore Carl hadn't done it. The prosecutor had to prove the murder had taken place. He had no toxicological evidence for Marge's story of a succinylcholine injection, but he did have evidence of the fractured larynx, which was passed among the jurors.

Using the hell-hath-no-fury approach, Bailey demolished Marge. "This woman drips with venom," he said; her story was a web of lies, the rantings of a woman scorned. Then he dealt with Milton Helpern, who was unaccustomed to being dealt with. Helpern had made slides of the colonel's coronary arteries and was planning to show a few of them to the jury to prove the colonel didn't die of heart disease. Bailey thought the jury should not be deprived of the benefit of all seventy-five of them, and insisted that Helpern show every last one. Using an old, cumbersome projector, Helpern had to explain away all the abnormalities in the colonel's arteries, one after another—this narrowing doesn't matter, that spot is unimportant and had nothing to do with his death, on and on for over an hour. The slide show succeeded in convincing the jury that Farber had heart disease.

The larynx remained. Bailey found two experts who thought the fracture was postmortem, an accidental blow inflicted by a gravedigger's shovel. This was very questionable, considering that the colonel was in a coffin when he was dug up. True, the sides of the coffin and the outer box had collapsed, but the inner lining surrounding the colonel was intact. But Bailey pulled it off, and Carl was acquitted of the murder of Colonel Farber.

For the second trial, the murder of Carmela in Sarasota, Bailey was a little too sure of himself. He had asked for a change of venue, hoping for the big-city sophistication of Miami, but he got the wrong venue. He got Naples, Florida, which was even smaller and more rural than Sarasota. He spent a lot of time with reporters, flying around the state in his Learjet. Frank Schaub, the prosecutor, was his antagonist in every sense. Schaub was a slow, deliberate talker who dressed badly and shuffled when he walked. Bailey was quicksilver, electricity. They were like the tortoise and the hare.

In Carmela's case, there was no backup fractured larynx. The critical question was the presence or absence of succinylcholine in the body.

Helpern was certain that Coppolino was guilty. The prosecutor had looked into his background at Methodist Hospital in Brooklyn, where he had worked previously, and learned that he had left under unsavory circumstances. The police had traced anonymous letters to him. He had sent them to a nurse, threatening to mutilate her if she continued to work in the hospital. He was jealous that she was taking away his patients. The hospital, not anxious to be caught in a scandal, let him resign. Shortly afterward, he declared himself disabled from a heart condition and began to live on his disability insurance. After that piece of information, we thought we'd see if anything had happened to any of his patients. We found an inordinate number of operative deaths that had never been reported, but there was no way to prove anything. There are surgical deaths and anesthesiological deaths. When a patient dies during an operation, the surgeon may call it an anesthesiological death, and the anesthetist may call it a surgical death. The hospital, desirous of avoiding lawsuits, says as little as possible.

Given Carl's background, Helpern believed the worst and thought he could find traces of this virtually undetectable poison. The breakdown products, succinic acid and choline, are normally present in the body. You have to find an excess. Helpern's chief toxicologist, Joseph Umberger, found the products, and Helpern testified that the amount in Carmela's brain was larger than normal. But Bailey charged that the tests had been conducted in secret, and the results were wrong. Three of the toxicologists who had worked on them agreed with Bailey. Helpern forced them out. Did anyone really know the normal amount of succinic acid and choline in a brain that had been buried for six months? It became a question of which toxicologist the jury would believe. Bailey's man, Dr. Francis Foldes, who found only normal amounts of the breakdown, was chief of anesthesiology at Montefiore Hospital and an expert on the subject. He had introduced succinylcholine into this country. He was a German refugee and spoke with an accent. Umberger, a farm boy from Oklahoma, did not seem to take himself seriously. He dressed in baggy pants and tobacco-stained shirt and carried an ancient, bulging briefcase. He looked like an alien among the suits of New York. As he walked in, chewing tobacco, his briefcase overflowing, he stopped and winked at the jurors. They cracked up. He looked like them; they recognized him as one of their kind, and they believed him. Coppolino was found guilty and given a life sentence, but he served only twelve and a half years of it. Now, almost a quarter of a century has passed, and his heart disease seems to have disappeared with age, reversing the usual process. His license to practice medicine was revoked, but he found something else to do. He consults.

He reviews cases and finds doctors who serve as witnesses at trials. He has become an expert.

While Carl Coppolino was trying out his skills with succinylcholine, Dr. Mario E. Jascalevich, another charming solipsist, was working with curare. Jascalevich was an Argentinian, born in 1927 in Buenos Aires. During the 1960s he invented a surgical stapler that carries his name. With the exception of euthanasia deaths, his was the first significant case in which a doctor was tried for intentionally killing patients who were also strangers. He was accused of murdering the patients of other doctors in his hospital to make himself look better. As doubt grew about their abilities, the money they earned from consultations would flow to him.

From 1963 to 1968 Dr. Jascalevich was the chief surgeon and the only one with full privileges at Riverdell Hospital, a small private hospital in Oradell, New Jersey. He was not popular with his peers. Other doctors complained how grudging he was with help. When they needed to consult with him on surgical problems—the treatment for abdominal pain, or a blood clot—he either wasn't available or he didn't respond quickly enough. In 1966 the hospital board brought in another surgeon, Dr. Robert Briski, an osteopath. Briski was helpful, cooperative, and available when needed, and he brought in his own patients. For a time, the board was delighted. Then something odd began to happen. Inexplicably, Briski's patients started dying after simple, routine operations—gall bladder, appendix. It was embarrassing. Within a year his privileges were restricted to minor surgery, like hernias, with someone watching. Briski was shattered. He thought he was jinxed.

A few months after Briski joined the staff, and over Jascalevich's objections, the board had brought in another general surgeon, Dr. Stanley Harris, whose specialty was vascular surgery. Soon his patients started to die, too, at the incredible rate of two or three a month. Harris couldn't imagine what was causing all these deaths. The autopsy results were vague—the deaths were attributed to various postoperative complications or heart attacks. Suddenly they stopped, and he relaxed. Then early one morning the hospital called to tell him that another of his patients had died. He rushed over and noticed that Jascalevich was there. Jascalevich had been on vacation for several weeks. Harris, who was more tough-minded than Briski, realized that none of his patients had died during the time Jascalevich was away. And now, just days after Jascalevich had returned, someone was dead. There was a notation on the patient's chart that Jascalevich had visited him. Harris thought it odd. He hadn't been asked to, and there was no reason for it. Harris thought he was on to something. He looked through the records of his other dead patients, and sure enough, Jascalevich had visited every one of them before they died. The visits violated protocol. Harris went to Dr. Allan Lans, a member of the hospital's board of directors.

The Coppolino case was making headlines, and succinylcholine was on everyone's mind. Lans thought Jascalevich might have been using it. He and Harris and other members of the board confronted Jascalevich and opened his locker. Inside they found needles, syringes, and eighteen vials of curare. The vials were almost empty.

The next day the board took its suspicions to Guy Calissi, the DA. Doctors almost never bring charges against each other to outside authorities. They had to be very certain of Jascalevich's guilt for them to go this far. Calissi and his assistant, Fred Galda, seized the contents of Jascalevich's locker and questioned him. Jascalevich handled them with a combination of charm and threats. He said he would resign but not under a cloud and not if the newspapers picked up the story and made him look guilty. Everything had to be kept quiet. He had a perfectly innocent explanation for the curare. He experimented on dogs at a medical school and used curare as an anesthesia. For the rest, he stonewalled. People die of "an undetermined physiological reaction," he said of a dead child; it could happen to anyone.

Three months later, Calissi and Galda ended their investigation and cleared Jascalevich. They didn't check the dog story or make the connection with Coppolino and his cat story. Jascalevich resigned and Harris succeeded him. There were no more suspicious deaths.

Over the next ten years, rumors kept bobbing up about a terrible secret harbored by the hospital—that thirty or forty people had been murdered and it had been covered up. From time to time a reporter would look into it, but nothing came of it until 1975, when Myron Farber at the *New York Times* became intrigued. The odds were against him. It was not to the advantage of certain interests to reopen the case. The DA and his assistant had become judges; the hospital board of directors were community pillars, and the doctors who issued the original death certificates would want to defend their diagnoses. They would become allied with the defense. A new investigation would cast a cloud on all of them.

Farber found a secret source (he later went to jail to protect the source's name) who gave him access to the old records. He went to the medical school where the animal experiments were supposed to have taken place and learned that Jascalevich had never done any work there. It was all a lie. What was the curare for? He also got records from the DA's office. Twenty-five patients had died. Thirteen of them seemed more suspicious than the rest. The chart of each had a notation that Jascalevich had been their angel of expiration—he had visited them just before they took their last breath. None was a patient of Jascalevich's. Some of them were dying of serious illnesses—cancer, heart disease. Of the thirteen, nine looked most likely to have been helped into their graves—the deaths were sudden and not in keeping with the nature of their illness. There was no cause that could compete with poisoning.

Farber presented the findings to the Bergen County prosecutor, Joe Woodcock, who asked me to review the cases for him. The New Jersey MEs who would normally have done it were compromised. Both Edwin Albano, the statewide ME, and Lawrence Denson, the Bergen County ME, had been among the original investigators who had accepted the deaths as innocent. Woodcock assigned a junior person to it, assistant DA Sybil Moses (now a judge). The case had been lying around for a decade; nobody thought it would go anywhere.

There wasn't enough evidence to force an exhumation of any of the patients, but five families agreed to it. It could not have been done without their consent. Other newspapers got wind of the story, but their ability to use it was limited—no one could print Jascalevich's name because he had not been officially charged and could have sued for libel. To protect his reputation, the press referred to him as "Dr. X." Everyone involved in the case knew who he was—everyone except the public who needed to know the most.

The first body we exhumed was that of Nancy Savino, a four-year-old child, buried for ten years. She had seemed to be recovering after having her appendix removed, but then had died suddenly. The hospital did an autopsy, but no one could explain it. The death certificate said "cause undetermined."

The gravediggers went to the cemetery at 7:30 A.M., which is the normal time to dig up bodies. The main reason is economic. If the body can be dug up, examined, and returned to its grave the same day, it costs less. It's also less harrowing emotionally for the family. Exhuming a body that is ten years dead is a highly dramatic thing to do. Usually, an exhumation is done a few weeks, or at most a year, after death, the time during which questions about a case arise. It was winter. Snow was on the ground, and fresh flowers lay at the headstones. The gravediggers used a backhoe to break through the frozen topsoil. It took a couple of hours, but we were lucky. The casket had been put into a cement vault which keeps water out. Nancy Savino's parents had also chosen a metal casket for her. It hadn't cracked and it was still sealed tight. Cast-iron caskets were used in the Civil War. When some of them were opened up a century later, the bodies were still in good shape—some had recognizable features and even internal organs. Many of the uniforms were preserved, and were taken out and put in museums. Nancy Savino's gravediggers pulled up her casket with loops of heavy cloth, and we brought it to our Decomposed Room. Everything depended on the condition of the body. Would the specimens be good enough for the toxicology lab? Curare concentrates in the cartilage of animals, and in the soft tissues that are among the earliest to decompose. But Nancy Savino had been embalmed, so there was a good chance we would find something.

The room was crowded. There were toxicologists to take specimens, a stenographer, two mortuary dieners (assistants to the pathologist who do such things as sew up the body), a photographer, Joe Woodcock (the Bergen County DA), and Edwin Albano (the Jersey ME). Beneath the facade of rational scientific inquiry, old resentments smoldered. Albano felt his turf had been invaded, and he was miffed that he hadn't been put in charge. Maybe people were saying that his first decision had been a whitewash, but still—it was a Jersey case, and why was it being done in New York City? He felt slighted. Helpern thought the whole thing was ridiculous, that after ten years there would be nothing but a putrid mess and a bag of bones. The press was skeptical. It was an election year in New Jersey and Woodcock might be running for governor. This looked like a publicity stunt. Suspicion and bitterness still lingered from the decade-old Coppolino case. Dr. Richard Coumbis, now chief toxicologist of New Jersey, had been one of those fired by Helpern for questioning his findings on the amount of succinylcholine in Carmela Coppolino's brain. Helpern had been accused of making the finding in secret, and here was another exotic poison that might be there or it might not, who could tell? To counter all this distrust, I wanted the exhumation and toxicology done in the open, in full view with everyone watching. No sleight-of-hand and no mirrors.

The moment of truth arrived. We uncranked the lid of the coffin and slowly lifted it up. No one in the room had ever seen a body that had been in the ground for ten years. There was a collective gasp as the lid was raised. Nancy Savino was most remarkably well preserved. The pink crinoline dress she had been buried in was clean and crisp. It looked starched. A cross and a withered rose lay on her chest, exactly as her parents had described them. The dryness had preserved everything. The organs and tissues could be analyzed.

By previous agreement, I divided the tissues among several toxicology labs in New Jersey, Long Island, and California. The eyes are particularly important in looking for poisons. Eye fluid (vitreous humor) is a place where they remain preserved. The eye contains about a tablespoon of fluid, like a little bag of water. The eye itself is a hollow organ and the fluid decomposes very slowly.

Dr. Richard Coumbis, the most skeptical of the toxicologists, who had specifically requested an eye, was the first to find curare. (What you actually find, using the gas chromatograph and mass spectrometer, are the molecular building blocks of the poison.) Then all the labs found it. We exhumed the other four bodies and found it in all of them. In the most decomposed body it was in the spinal cord.

The trial was presided over by Judge William J. Arnold. It was his last case before his retirement, and an awkward one for him. Two of his fellow judges were the Bergen County prosecutors who were being criticized for absolving Jascalevich in the original investigation. He had a nervous rash on his hands. All during the trial he wore rubber gloves and kept picking at them. I could hear him plucking away when I was on the stand. Other difficulties plagued him. He had trouble remembering the lawyers' names. He frequently had his eyes closed and seemed to be napping. The prosecutor thought he was biased in favor of

Jascalevich and asked him to disqualify himself, an unusual move for a lawyer to make against the judge who holds the fate of a client in his hands. He refused.

After thirty-five weeks of testimony, it took the jury less than three hours to come back with an acquittal. The defense attorney, Raymond A. Brown, understood that in a long trial a relationship develops between the jurors and the defendant. He grasped the value of personal connections and paid attention to details. Jascalevich dressed well and said good morning to the jury. He was friendly; he thanked me for my testimony even though I was on the other side. He greeted witnesses and said goodbye to them and expressed his gratitude to them when they left, like a good host. He kissed several of the women in the courtroom. Jascalevich ran a clinic for people on welfare, and many of his clients, who were not working, packed the courtroom and applauded him. The jury was so dazzled by his performance that they later sent a letter to Albano, expressing their outrage that the good doctor's medical license had not been restored to him after the trial. Jascalevich had voluntarily surrendered it at the time of the indictment.

But there was good cause. The New Jersey Medical Licensing Board had been investigating him for other reasons. Apart from his indictment for killing five patients with curare, the board charged him with seven counts of malpractice, including operating for cancer on a patient who didn't have the disease, fraud, and neglect. These therapeutic misdemeanors took place at another hospital in Jersey City where he had operating privileges. In 1980 his license was revoked permanently.

But Jascalevich knew when he was ahead. He skipped the country in 1981 and returned to Argentina, leaving the insurance companies holding the bag for malpractice charges. Raymond Brown, the defense attorney who had done such a wonderful job for him, wasn't paid either. Dr. X died in Mar del Plata, Argentina, in 1984, at age fifty-seven. Riverdell Hospital changed its name twice after the trial, but anonymity eluded it. It finally shut down for lack of patients. People felt nervous about going there.

10

CLOSE CALLS

ACCIDENTAL DEATH

ON MARCH 11, 1971, Whitney Young, the executive director of the National Urban League, died in Lagos, Nigeria. He had been attending an Afro-American conference with Ramsey Clark, the former U.S. Attorney General, and Percy Sutton, the former Manhattan borough president, among others. He was swimming in the ocean in rough surf about one hundred feet from shore when he collapsed. His friends, who were standing on the beach, saw his arm go up and his head go down before he went under. Clark, who was swimming with him, pulled him out of the water. His friends worked on him for over an hour with his head lower than his feet, but it was too late.

Young was autopsied in a Lagos hospital. The doctor reported that he had died of a brain hemorrhage, and returned the body to New York in a wooden casket with a metal liner. The death certificate came with the body, along with a description of the death. By international agreement, all countries have to supply a document stating that the death was not caused by a contagious disease. People who die of something contagious, like yellow fever, in a foreign country, can't leave—they must be buried or cremated there.

The family was not satisfied with the diagnosis. After it became public knowledge, rumors began circulating that Young had been killed. Even though he had been swimming in plain view of the whole beach, the diagnosis of brain hemorrhage had raised the possibility that someone had hit him on the head. Why else would he have a hemorrhage around his brain? The causes of a brain hemorrhage could be unnatural as well as natural. He was a good swimmer, so drowning was unlikely. Maybe there was a cover-up.

Dr. Allan Dumont, the family physician, called me. He was a surgeon and professor at Bellevue who had been one of my teachers. The family wanted another autopsy. When I opened the metal liner, the body was in good condition, embalmed and dressed with the two traditional sutured incisions. The usual procedure is to take the organs out, inspect them, and dissect them. The Nigerians had touched nothing. All the organs were in place, just as they had been in life. A towel had been put beneath the skin to soak up fluids. The brain was congested and reddish, and I took it out. Except for the color, it was normal. There was no injury and no hemorrhage. The lungs were more difficult to call. You don't always see water in the lungs in a drowning, and when you do, the fluid is the same as the fluid from a heart attack. There's no label on it, indicating point of origin. But there was sand and seaweed in the windpipe and sand in the bronchi, which was very persuasive evidence to me that Young had inhaled water and drowned. He also had an enlarged heart and a history of high blood pressure. It was a very hot day in Lagos, and bad hearts get into trouble in extremes of weather. I thought the heat had brought on cardiac arrhythmia. If he had been at home in bed and been treated he would have survived it; instead, it precipitated his drowning.

I found out later how the Nigerian autopsy had been done. The doctor had misinterpreted the reddishness around the brain.

It was due to gravity, not a blow. Young had been lying on the beach with his head lower than his feet while his friends tried to save him. Blood rushed to his brain, making it look as if he had hemorrhaged. The Nigerians had also practiced the hands-off policy that goes into effect around the world when an important foreigner dies. Important foreigners get special treatment. Corners are cut for them, which often serves to make the death look suspicious whether it is or not. In this death there were political nuances and media attention to consider, as well as the family's feelings. The Nigerians were sensitive to all of it. First, they contacted the American embassy. The embassy was not anxious to have an autopsy done—families don't usually want one—and sent its own doctor, a general practitioner, to observe the Nigerian ME. The American didn't really understand what he was seeing, but he represented the family's interests, and his presence should have permitted the ME to do everything he needed to do. The ME, though, saw things from another angle. He considered himself to be working under the guidance of the Americans, and assumed that everyone would be happier if he did the minimum necessary. If he had done a full autopsy and come up with a reasonable cause, the family would have been satisfied. It was just a case of good intentions and bad communications.

Late one April night in 1988, Robert Travis, Jr., twenty-five years old, and his seventeen-year-old cousin, Larry Peters, Jr., drove to the big mansion on the hill, the estate in Cambridge, New York, where they worked, to steal a little gasoline. It was a lark, a Tom Sawyerish prank, no malice intended. Travis didn't have enough money to buy gas. He and his cousin were the kind of people the police called "mullies," or "dirtbags," or "woodchucks"—rural people who grew up poor and ignorant, who wore the same dirty jeans covered with oil stains day after day, people who were constitutionally unable to stay out of trouble.

The estate belonged to Dr. Josephine Wells Brown, a seventy-six-year-old retired radiologist. Her husband, also a doctor, was dead, and she lived alone in a three-story redbrick Georgian house with fireplaces at each end. The estate was in a remote area near Glens Falls, and was virtually self-sufficient—she grew food and had her own generator and a gasoline pump for the farm equipment. She was an animal lover and kept registered quarter horses. Antiques were one of her interests—the house was filled with them, and she ran an antiques shop on the property. Around town she was regarded as something of a character for being outspoken and demanding and for devoting herself so wholeheartedly to her horses, but she was well liked.

Dr. Brown kept the farm going with a combination of house servants and field labor. She hired hourly farm workers (the only kind available) from the local population. Travis and Peters and a third man, Mark Dickinson, did the yard and stable work and were not allowed into the house. Dr. Brown kept the inside and outside people carefully separated. On payday, the outside workers went to a wooden shed in back of the house that opened into the kitchen and were given checks. Dr. Brown didn't keep cash in the house. She was afraid. A few days before her death she confided to a friend that she was particularly afraid of Travis, whose nickname was Matches. In his youth he had once burned down someone's barn.

On this particular day, Travis and Peters, who was somewhat dim-witted, were working together on Peters's grandfather's tractor. Peters lived with his grandfather. Travis, in a spirit of fun, suggested that they find some excitement that night, that they go out and drink wine coolers and smoke cigarettes. This was an adventurous thing for them to be doing. Their lives were narrow and their days repetitious.

That night, Peters sneaked out the window and met his cousin. After buying orange wine coolers and cigarettes, Travis had no money left to buy gas and decided to siphon some from Dr. Brown's pump. It was another daring thing to do.

They drove to the farm in Travis's half-wrecked 1973 Chevrolet with its unmatched doors from different cars, rusting and filthy. They went halfway up the driveway that circled the house, turned off their lights, and stopped, fearful of being seen. Upstairs, lights were still on. They sat for an hour, waiting. After a while the lights went out, and they drove the Chevy in the dark around to the rear of the house where the gas pump and antiques shop were.

Dr. Brown had left the night lights on near the pump, and Travis thought he'd better turn them off. The car could be seen in the light. But he could only do it by turning off the circuit breaker, which was inside the wooden shed, and he was too short to reach it. While Peters waited in the car, Travis went to look for a stool or a ladder to stand on. He had something else on his mind, too—Dr. Brown's rifle. He knew she had one, and he wanted to steal it. It's unclear where he thought she kept it. From interviews with Travis, the prosecutor had the impression that he thought she kept it outside her bedroom door. Travis was ignorant of her habits, too. Dr. Brown was accustomed to sleeping for a few hours after dinner, and then getting up to wander around the house. She was a night owl.

Travis opened the door that led to the kitchen and saw Dr. Brown standing there in a pink nightgown, holding the coveted rifle. She had known they were there. She had seen the car but hadn't wanted to go outside and confront them. Her worst fear was coming true. "What do you want?" she said. Travis was so startled he instinctively struck out, punching her in the neck. She collapsed instantly. He searched for a pulse but couldn't find one and decided she was dead.

He sat there for a while, trying to figure out what to do. He hadn't meant to kill her, and in a way it wasn't really his fault; so maybe the best thing would be to destroy the evidence. Given his past experience, the way to do that was to burn down the house. He went back outside and told Peters that he had found Dr. Brown lying there dead, but he knew exactly what to do—

she had once asked him to burn the house down if he ever found her dead. Peters helped him torch the house.

Travis carried the body into the living room and laid it in front of one of the fireplaces. He found a gasoline container and poured kerosene and gasoline through the house, around the body, and all over the Oriental rugs. He had found some gloves, but even so he burned his hand. Arson is tricky. Gasoline evaporates at a very low temperature. After pouring it, if you wait a few minutes to light a match, enough vapor may rise to create an oxygen-gasoline mixture that explodes—a fireball. Often in arson cases, the cops' best leads come out of the local emergency room, where people with burns on their hands or faces have gone to be treated. A more experienced arsonist would have started the fire from a distance, using a rope or a cord, and he would not have waited long enough for the gasoline to evaporate.

With the house beginning to blaze behind them, Travis and Peters drove back to town to arrange their alibis. Peters sneaked back through his grandfather's window. Travis arrived a few minutes later. He called Mark Dickinson, the third field hand, and told him they were needed on a rescue mission: Dr. Brown had just telephoned him for help. The fire in her fireplace was getting out of hand and she needed him to put it out. He didn't want to go alone, and he would pick up his friend on the way.

The next day in Peters's school, everyone was talking about the big fire at Dr. Brown's place and how she had died in it. It was the most exciting thing to happen in Cambridge in ages. Peters went to the infirmary to have the bandage changed on an old injury, and even there it was the main topic of conversation. He was one up on everyone, and he contributed to the excitement by telling the nurse that he had been at Dr. Brown's house the night before. After hearing this electrifying piece of news, the nurse called Peters's mother, who called the sheriff, who called the DA, and before he knew what was happening, Peters was sitting in the DA's office being questioned. He spent the whole day telling his story, gradually getting himself in deeper and deeper. At first he said he had had nothing to do with it; he was only there because his cousin had asked him. But he was very suggestible, and by the end of the day he admitted that he had seen Dr. Brown dead before the fire started and had incriminated his cousin.

Dr. Wong Ham Lee, the local pathologist, did the postmortem at Glens Falls Hospital. Travis had made the mistake of assuming the fire would destroy all signs of Dr. Brown's death, but it isn't easy to destroy a body. Flesh doesn't burn spontaneously, and kerosene gets used up very quickly. If a lit match falls on dead skin, it will go out. In a fire, people die of carbon monoxide poisoning and soot inhalation. After they are unconscious or dead, they may be burned, but the fire has to be fueled by something other than skin—by clothing, or a wooden floor.

The first order of business was to identify the body. You can't automatically assume that the body in the building belongs there. Dr. Brown had patches of unmarked skin. She was lying on the floor on her back. The ceiling had collapsed on her front, burning her badly, but she was not burned on her back, on the places where her body was pressed against the floor and no oxygen reached. From the skin we knew she was white, which was a start. As always, the most reliable way to identify the dead woman was through X rays and teeth. One particular tooth had had extensive root-canal work done on it. It was conclusive.

As is routine in a fire death, Dr. Lee tested for carbon monoxide. Finding none, he concluded that Dr. Brown hadn't breathed in any poisonous fumes and was dead when the fire started. But he also saw soot in the windpipe, which meant exactly the opposite—that she *had* breathed in smoke and was therefore alive when the fire started. So it looked like an accident—death from smoke inhalation. But there was also her head to consider. It looked as if she had a subdural hemorrhage around the brain, meaning that Dr. Brown had been hit on the head and died of a fractured skull and brain injury. That made her death a murder. Murder meant arson—she couldn't have died and then started the fire after she was dead. But the fire marshals had looked for accelerants and found no evidence of arson. When accelerants like gasoline and kerosene evaporate, they produce hydrocarbons (compounds made of hydrogen and carbon) that have a low molecular weight. But when wood burns, it produces heavier hydrocarbons. The marshals could find only the heavier hydrocarbons, and concluded the fire was an accident.

All this added up to complete confusion. Every sign pointed to something different. Travis had confessed, but the police were having a hard time believing him. His confession did not bear out Lee's finding of soot inhalation. They dug out Travis's file and found the barn burning, but they hesitated. The police are very reluctant to say a death in a fire is murder because arson is hard to prove, and they have to prove arson to prove murder. The fire marshals went back for a second look. Part of the problem with hydrocarbons is their volatility. They are hard to find. The winds just blow them away. This time the marshals looked under the rug, in clothing, in corners, and found low-weight gasoline hydrocarbons. It was arson.

Now the police had to find out whether Dr. Brown was dead when the fire started. Travis said yes and the subdural hemorrhage said yes, but that meant two different causes. The soot in the windpipe said no, but the lack of carbon monoxide said yes. Which was it? They called to run the findings by me—were they consistent with a possible homicide? I said they couldn't have it both ways—if they had soot they had to have carbon monoxide too. I reautopsied the body with Lee and found that the subdural hemorrhage was really an epidural hemorrhage—it was just under the skull. Dr. Brown had not been hit on the head. The injury was caused by the fire itself, after death. Fire has an immense destructive power. It tightens and tears the skin like a knife wound. It makes the blood in the bones boil so that they fracture and break apart. Part of the skull was found a distance away from the body.

I looked at the blood for the telltale pink of carbon monoxide.

It wasn't there. I looked at the lungs for soot and found none. Therefore, she had already been dead. The soot in the windpipe was a very small amount near the top and had been washed in after death. It came from the water the firemen had been pouring on the fire. Then I looked at the heart and saw a very severe case of hardening of the arteries. As a cause of death, that fit Travis's confession—he punched her and she collapsed and died. In cases of advanced heart disease, heavy physical exertion or a powerful surge of emotion, like rage or fear, can trigger a precipitous drop in the blood flow to the heart. The amount of oxygen being pumped kept diminishing until it was too little to keep her alive. The punch was the *coup de grace.*

At the autopsy, there was no evidence of the punch. All of Dr. Brown's injuries were due to the fire. Neither the police nor the DA was happy with my conclusions. My postmortem converted a simple homicide which pleased everyone into one that was complicated and difficult to understand. It was still a homicide—Travis's blow was responsible for her death—but it was indirect. It would have been easier to prosecute an obvious smash-on-the-head murder and a vicious killer.

The case is awaiting trial, and Peters and Travis are in jail. The lawyers worked out a plea bargain for Peters, but it fell apart. As one of the prosecutors said, he should be convicted of "public imbecility."

In the following story, which took place on Maui, the dates and some names have been changed to protect the family.

On the day of her death, Daphne Mellon spent most of the afternoon with her sister, Laura. They shopped at the Moon Bow boutique on Papalaua Street, where Daphne bought a black dress. Afterward they got a root beer at the McDonald's at the corner of Wainee and Papalaua streets. Daphne called her boyfriend, Matthew Privlin, and Laura overheard her telling him she would pick him up at 9:00 at the restaurant where he worked as a cook. That night Daphne drove her Toyota to Maui Community College, where she was taking a summer course in history. Her class ended at 8:30, and she planned to spend half an hour in the Kaoahumanu shopping center before meeting Matt. She never arrived. At about 9:30 or so, Matt called Priscilla Mellon, Daphne's mother, to tell her that Daphne hadn't shown up. He drank two bottles of beer in the bar and went home at 10:30, and then called again. He went to sleep at 2:00 A.M. Daphne didn't come home that night.

Early the next morning, Priscilla Mellon reported her daughter missing to the police. Shortly afterward, a stranger called to tell her that Daphne's wallet and car registration papers were scattered on the road in front of his house. Laura and Matt went. Driving along the Honoapiilani Highway, they saw Daphne's car parked on the shoulder. It was out of gas.

Daphne's partially decomposed body was found in the middle of a sugar-cane field on July 8, 1986. She was twenty years old and had last been seen alive three days before, leaving Maui Community College. If it hadn't been for the three teenagers who came to check on their marijuana plants, she would not have been discovered. Cane grows to a height of eight feet and is extremely dense. It wasn't due to be harvested for months.

After the body was discovered, Dr. Roger Kerris autopsied it and signed it off as "undetermined." Kerris was the ME of Oahu, but Maui didn't have an ME of its own, and every so often Kerris flew over to help. He couldn't find anything wrong—no disease, no injury, no sign of drugs or alcohol. There was semen in Daphne's vagina, but no indication of violence. Dr. Frank Bronson at the G.N. Wilcox Memorial Hospital and Health Care Center on Maui did the toxicology tests. He didn't find anything either. But Kerris didn't quite believe his findings. How could a healthy twenty-year-old woman have died of nothing? She was wearing very little—underpants and a shirt—and no shoes. Friends remembered that she had been dressed in a white ruffled shirt, a tie-dyed miniskirt, a sash, and sandals. And there was the matter of her car. It had been found a few miles along the road from the body, and the license and registration and wallet were found a few miles beyond that. Kerris thought the whole setup looked like murder, and the police thought so, too. She could have run out of gas and been picked up by her killer, who robbed her and got rid of her wallet at the nearest convenient place. Kerris didn't have any medical evidence to support his theory, but he wrote on the autopsy report that Daphne Mellon was probably raped and either strangled or suffocated.

(Not long after Daphne's death, Kerris returned to Louisiana, where he had come from. He was called back to Hawaii to testify in a battered-child case in which the defense claimed that the child's death from a fractured skull was unintentional: the baby had been dropped accidentally on his head. Kerris testified that a baby can't get that kind of fracture from being dropped on its head, and in an extraordinary lapse of judgment he told people that he had prepared for his testimony by getting some dead babies and dropping them on their heads. The babies had recently died from sudden infant death syndrome. Their parents had not been consulted about their participation in this experiment. In the ensuing pandemonium, Kerris fell from grace and was told that the demand for his services in Louisiana had diminished.)

Daphne's parents were distraught. They wanted the police to arrest Matt, but he had an unbreakable alibi. He had been working until 9:00, and the manager of the restaurant verified his story of sitting at the bar waiting for Daphne.

Matt and his mother and brothers had moved to Maui from Los Angeles after his mother's divorce. He had dropped out of school and gone to work to supplement her income. He and Daphne had dated on and off for two years, he told the police. They had had an affair, but she backed off when he offered to buy her an engagement ring. She was getting her degree at the University of Hawaii on Oahu. During the school year she slept with fifteen members of the football team and told Matt about it. He was fascinated. It excited him enormously. A central part of their relationship consisted of him asking her to describe the whole thing in graphic detail and her telling him. He would then get angry and say it was disgusting and she would cry. Then they would make up. The police were suspicious that he might have killed her in a fit of jealousy, but Matt had another candidate—Joseph Orami, a former classmate.

The night before her death, Daphne and Matt had gone to the Banana Moon disco at the Marriott Hotel. At around 10:00, Joseph had come to their table and said something crude about Daphne's body. Matt told him to buzz off. Joseph told the police that he didn't remember saying anything offensive, just "Hey, you got one nice old lady." Whatever it was that he said, the police didn't think he had killed Daphne. They gave him a lie detector test, and he passed. But because of the brief time of only half an hour (8:30–9:00) that Daphne was missing, the police thought a lot of people were lying. Matt, for one, might know much more than he was telling. He wouldn't finish his polygraph test and left the island because, he said, the police were pestering him.

The cause of Daphne's death remained a mystery for two years. In 1988 I was asked to evaluate several cases that the Maui police hadn't been able to solve. When I looked over the reports on Daphne, I picked up tantalizing hints of drugs that trailed off into nowhere. Daphne had bought $100 worth of cocaine from an acquaintance who worked at the Maui Horse Center, and a razor blade with cocaine residue was found in her car. The toxicology report was negative, so no one thought it mattered. One interview followed the thread—Detective Robert Tam Ho's talk with Alison Monk, one of Daphne's college friends. Alison had heard a rumor from Matt, who got it from someone he refused to identify, that Daphne had died at a party while freebasing cocaine. Her friends had panicked and moved the body to avoid being incriminated, not realizing that people would think it was murder. The police discounted Alison's story (where did this mythical party take place, and who was there?), but to me it rang true. It looked like the same old streets-of-New York kind of incident that I'd been dealing with for much of my career. In big cities the police call it "dumping," but wherever it happens it's the same thing. Someone overdoses unexpectedly in the wrong place, with the wrong people, and the body is an embarrassment. They don't have time, they don't want to be bothered with police procedures; these are not the kind of people to get involved in a sordid little episode, and they certainly don't want anyone to know they've been doing drugs. It's much easier to move the body somewhere else and go on with their lives.

Daphne's friends were amateurs, which is why the scene looked like murder. Amateurs always cause confusion. They don't realize the consequences of what they are doing. They had taken her body to the sugar-cane fields (an excellent hiding place) and then driven her car north and abandoned it when it ran out of gas. It could have been burglarized by anyone walking along the highway, who then discarded the wallet.

As for Daphne's wearing only a shirt and underpants, that reinforced the idea of a cocaine and sex party. Her shoes could have been left in the apartment where she died. There was no hyoid fracture, no sign of any violence—the only thing left was drugs.

Although the hospital toxicology tests were negative, I knew that I couldn't always believe everything I read in an autopsy report. The equipment at Wilcox Hospital, where the tests were done, was all right for analyzing urine, but not autopsy tissues. Without high-tech equipment, cocaine can't be found in a decomposed body. After death the enzymes continue to break it down, hydrolizing it into benzoylecgonine, which is even harder to find.

Now it was two years later, but I thought the ME's office might have saved the frozen tissues and body fluids. But the office was in disarray—nothing was left. I tried Wilcox Hospital.

Hospitals don't usually save this material for two years, but Daphne Mellon had been an unusual case for them. Wilcox normally did urine screening on addicts, and if there was any problem with the specimen, the addicts could always come back. Daphne was different—she was a murder, or so they thought. They rarely got the opportunity to examine decomposed tissues from a murder. There would be no second chance, and they had no authorization to throw out anything. So they saved it.

I mailed the fluids to Professor Randall Baselt, a forensic toxicologist and director of the Chemical Toxicology Institute in Foster City, California—a private lab that specializes in drugs in general and cocaine in particular. He found benzoylecgonine.

That gave us a cause of death but no satisfactory explanation of what had happened—only the whisper of a party that no one on Maui admits to having attended or even to knowing that it took place. Daphne's parents at first refused to countenance the idea of a drug overdose. The family was certain she had been murdered. To them, a murder was more comforting. A drug overdose was personal—to some degree it could be blamed on them. A murder was impersonal. A maniac was out there in the indifferent universe. Every time a young woman was murdered on Maui, they thought her killer might be the same one who killed Daphne, and they asked the police to investigate where he had been when Daphne died. Nothing ever turned up, and finally they became reconciled to the idea of a drug overdose. Priscilla Mellon was angry and bitter at Daphne's "friends," whoever they might be, who dumped her daughter's body so unceremoniously and left it to rot, just to save their own skins. But then one day a young woman was found on a beach on the other side of the island, and it started all over again. Mrs. Mellon called the police. Was there any possibility the same man could have killed Daphne?

Deaths during sexual misadventure are few in number and highly dramatic. They are almost always unintended. There are exceptions, like the man who had a heart attack while making love to his Electrolux, but usually it's a matter of being carried away by an overabundance of rapture and not noticing that the mechanism of joy has developed a kink. Risk taking is part of the thrill—the risk of tightening the rope, of being found out, of allowing yourself to be controlled by someone else. To an outsider, the deaths look like something else, like suicide or murder. The S&M practitioners and the solo performers who have rigged up elaborate contraptions to refine their pleasure look like the victims of a ritual killing carried out by a secret barbarian sect. Sometimes the scene has been dismantled and the victim dressed, making the death that much harder to explain, but under the clothes the body is bruised and bloody, and there are ligature marks around the neck that look like strangulation. The trappings confuse the issue and make it easy to misinterpret the manner of death—whether it is an accident, suicide, or murder.

The "suicides" are the adolescent boys—and an occasional girl—who have inadvertently hanged themselves while experimenting with new sensations. They have discovered that pressure on the carotid artery, cutting off the supply of oxygen to the brain, heightens the pleasure of orgasm. The closer they are to unconsciousness, the greater their pleasure. The idea is to ejaculate at the moment of tightest pressure on the neck, when the least amount of oxygen is getting to the brain, and to release the pressure just before losing consciousness. But something goes wrong with the escape device—the rope slips or the zipper gets stuck or the slip knot tightens—and they lose consciousness before they can disentangle themselves. They are found hanging in a private, out-of-the-way place—an attic or a basement. The great majority are signed out as suicides, which plays havoc with the statistics of teenage deaths, but that's another problem.

There is some question whether the parents are aware of what was going on and, given two impossible choices, if they prefer the stigma of suicide to the shame of an autoerotic death. When I was still working under Helpern, the parents of a Harvard student came to us. The Boston ME had declared their son's death by hanging a suicide, and they couldn't accept it. It was out of character. They had had a good close relationship with him, and if he had been depressed and miserable enough to kill himself, they would have known about it. The idea of not knowing was profoundly disturbing to them. They brought the Boston autopsy report, the police report, and the photographs of the scene to us. The evidence was in the pictures. The boy's fly was open, and there was a mirror and a copy of *Playboy* opened to the centerfold where he could see it. These are the universal artifacts of this particular scene. If it isn't *Playboy,* it's a similar magazine. He had put a piece of cloth between his neck and the rope so there would be no marks afterward and no one would know. Suicides don't worry about marks. His parents were relieved to learn the truth. Sexual experimentation was something they could live with.

There is a continuum in these affairs. Those who experiment with simple hanging often move on to more complicated arrangements with ropes and chains, weights and pulleys, dildoes and handcuffs. Unlike most of the people I see, their homes are filled with books—Freud, de Sade, Genet, von Sacher-Masoch. They are educated, successful professionals—more than any other group, doctors and lawyers seem to have an affinity for this sort of thing. I saw my first one when I was still a medical student—a lawyer found dead at home, wearing women's clothes. He had attached a dildo device to a bicycle, a long pink broomstick padded with foam rubber. As he got more and more excited and pedaled faster and faster he lost control of the situation and the device perforated his colon. We had no trouble calling his death: he was alone, and from the way he was dressed it was clearly an accident. Some of his neighbors knew about his proclivities.

The Sutton Place banker was more problematical. The police thought it was murder. He was a thirty-five-year-old vice-president of a French bank who lived in a luxury high-rise apartment on Sutton Place South. His coworkers hadn't been able to reach him and called the police. He had been dead twenty-four hours when they arrived. They found him spread-eagled on the bed, held down with leather straps attached to chains. His left hand was unstrapped, as if he had been trying to free himself when he died. A camera was set up with a remote switch and a floodlight. There was nothing in the room that looked as if it had killed him. The police thought it might be a ritual murder or that he had picked up a gay in a bar who had tied him up and killed him. There was a lot of camera equipment in the bureau drawer, but they couldn't tell if anything had been stolen. He also had a supply of marijuana, heroin, and amyl nitrite, also known as poppers or snappers. It's a fancy version of nitroglycerine. You squeeze the glass capsule to break it, then inhale, and the result, presumably, is a spectacular orgasm. It works the same way as hanging, by diminishing the supply of oxygen going to the brain. He had not been alone. Later, the police saw the note from his companion. "Dear Robert," it said, "What a wild kafkaesque evening. My telephone number is ———. Your move. Marilyn."

I didn't think his death had any connection with the leather and chains. He had no marks on his neck, just on his wrists and ankles. At autopsy, his lungs were filled with fluid. He could have been suffocated intentionally, but other than the fluid, there was no sign of it. Underneath the outlandish trappings, it looked like a normal heroin overdose, and toxicology confirmed that it was. Marilyn, the woman who wrote the note, was not prosecuted. All the paraphernalia belonged to him, and the doorman said he had a lot of visitors. He didn't die from his sex life, and the DA was satisfied that death was unintentional.

The most difficult of these cases to call are those involving S&M. The death is usually the result of a small miscalculation—but whose? Because S&M requires two people, there is a possibility that the mistake was deliberate. An internist who taught and practiced at a major New York hospital kept a diary and considered writing a book about his experiences, but was concerned that it might affect his practice. He knew he would have to deny his authorship, not out of shame but economics—he would certainly lose his license to practice if anyone unmasked him. And he didn't want to become a writer—he just wanted to write about *this*. "This is it, the sum and substance of my fantasies, lived, acted out, intended, aborted, and otherwise," he wrote. He worried about the bruises, the discolorations on his arms that his colleagues noticed at work. Fortunately for him, it was the skiing season, and they drew the obvious, if incorrect, conclusion.

The doctor was a masochist, obsessed with bondage fantasies, but the nurse he lived with was not a sadist. She loved him, and the thought of hurting him horrified her, but she also wanted to make him happy. It took him a long time to persuade her to cater to his desires. For her first full-fledged effort she hired a professional sadist, someone who provided physical pain for a living. One day he came home for lunch and the nurse had a surprise for him. They had experimented a little, so she wasn't entirely ignorant of the procedure. She put her favorite pillowcase over his head—the one with the lavender and violets—and slipped something down his back. As he fumbled to find it, she handcuffed his hands behind him. He went along with it, amused at her "childish games," but when she was finished with the preliminaries he had a chain around his neck, locked tightly in place, a gag in his mouth, and another tight chain between his legs, also locked in place. He was standing on a wobbly stool (a piece of furniture he could not remember seeing in the apartment before), his neck chain hooked to the ceiling, worrying about how dangerous it was—if the stool tipped over, he would hang himself.

She left the room and put some music on, a Vivaldi flute concerto. It enraged him. "How could she do that with me in here like this? She had gone off her rocker. I feared her return. What was next?" More chains were next, but he had to wait for them.

Waiting was part of the torture. She would leave for a while, come back and add something or hurt him in a new way, and leave again. He hung there, his wrists and fingers numb, the fight slowly ebbing out of him. Half an hour later she came back and chained his ankles together.

Her next return was more frightening. Standing behind him, she lifted the pillowcase and suddenly pulled a tight stocking over his head down to his chin. He couldn't breathe; it was pressed tight against his nose. Quickly she snipped a hole in it with a pair of scissors. He felt a trickle on his lips. Had she cut his nose? He couldn't tell. Then she wrapped adhesive tape around his face, mummifying him. "The heat was incredible. . . . I wanted out. . . . My jaw ached from the pressure on my chin. The pressure on my eyeballs made red kaleidoscopes. I knew if I choked on that damn gag the only thing to save me was a tracheostomy." She pulled a mask over his head and laced it up. Part of the pleasure is fear of the unexpected. The mask enhanced the sense of mystery and anticipation, the feelings of helplessness and submissiveness, of being at someone else's mercy. But she had overdone it. "I pushed with my tongue to move the gag forward. If I let that damn thing go further back it would cut off my air completely. My tongue was wedged below the gag. I felt it slipping backwards. Where was she?"

He realized that she hadn't spoken to him since she had first put the pillowcase over his head. "Was it she or had she gotten one of those crazy lunatics from one of the S&M clubs to take over for her?" He hung by his wrists, aching, numb, his genitals wrapped around with ropes and chains, his toes just touching the floor. The stool had been taken away. He heard a new record—"Strauss. Richard. Johann would have been too ludicrous."

He couldn't communicate with her, couldn't get her to pay attention to his needs. "I wanted to tell her that I needed to talk to her, that she was hurting me. . . . The first lash across my shoulders felt good. She landed a few good ones across the backs of my knees that burned like fire. I squirmed sensually with the warm glow that enveloped my back and butt. I began to enjoy myself. The thongs clattered dryly on the floor and the door slammed. She knew it."

Then she came back. "The first blow was like a knife. . . . Something was running down my back. Blood. It was cool. Aagh. . . . Another blow. My breathing was heavy. I tried to calm myself. My body shook. I let the pain envelop me. The redness of my mind suffused throughout me. The burning extended from my genitals to my fingertips. . . . A red kaleidoscope. I was going higher and higher. Maybe I was going to die. I didn't mind. I writhed with the redness, stretching and shrugging, feeling the burning skin fill my mind with redness. . . . The blood surged. An orgasm of relief. My mind cleared. I hurt. I smiled. I needed the pain to stay alive."

This first episode was in the summer. Soon the nurse learned what he liked and she herself became proficient at doing it. Their last game took place just before Christmas 1969. The doctor came home for lunch. The nurse put the gag and hood on him, handcuffed, chained, and whipped him, and let him stay like that, wondering what might happen next. While he hung there she ran out to Alexander's to pick up a Christmas present for him. When she came back he was dead. She unchained him, removed the mask and gag, put him in bed, and called the police.

The police sent him to us. They didn't see any signs of violent death—no knife or gunshot wounds—but they thought it could have been a drug overdose. He was thirty-five years old and had no history of illness. Until the age of forty, more men and women die of unnatural causes than natural—of suicide, accident, murder, or an overdose. I saw whip marks, ligature marks on the wrists and ankles, and hemorrhages in the whites of the eyes. The penis seemed scrunched and wrinkled. The mouth had abrasions inside, and there were also tears in the anus. All the organs were normal, and there was no sign of a heart attack or drugs.

After a body goes to the ME, a relative or someone close to the family has to make an identification and sign a form. The nurse came, and we discussed the findings with her. She was more comfortable talking to us as doctors than to the police. She had made her lover happy, and she didn't feel she had done anything wrong. She left the chains with us. They were a reminder of him. We reconstructed his death from her story. The gag was too far back in his throat. With a gag, you can breathe through your nose, but if it goes back too far it obstructs the entire airway. We sometimes get this kind of death when elderly people are robbed in their homes. The thief ties them up and gags them, thinking someone will come and rescue them, but the gag has been thrust too far back. By the time they are found it is too late.

The nurse told us the doctor had liked the first experience so much that she had begun doing it for him. The periods of isolation, of wondering what would come next, were part of the joy of it, and so was the music. When the police asked her why she had left him alone she said, "Because he looked like he was having such a good time."

I signed him out as "asphyxia during sexual bondage," and forbore to classify the death in one of our usual cubbyholes—homicide, suicide, natural, accident. It didn't seem to fit anywhere. It was *sui generis*. My job was to figure out the cause, not whether the death was intentional. That was the DA's job. And there was an opening for a criminal theory. A scenario of sexual jealousy could be developed, and a nurse who knew physiology could place a gag a centimeter too far. The DA decided it was a homicide—the nurse had contributed to the death by leaving the apartment. Even with the doctor's consent, she had an obligation to stay. The case seemed awfully flimsy to me. I thought he was just playing it safe—five years down the line no one could come back and say he had missed a murder. The grand jury decided not to indict. They thought it was disgusting and obscene, but the doctor and nurse were consenting adults; no one had been forced. The DA seemed satisfied with the decision.

11

DIAGNOSTIC FOLLIES

NATURAL ENDINGS

MANY OF THE cases I am asked to review hinge on the possibility of a mistaken diagnosis. In a murder, medical examiners who can't figure out the cause of death tend to go along with the police theory. Instead of arriving at their own independent conclusion, MEs just become rubber stamps. There is nothing deliberately dishonest about this. The police want to solve the murder, and the ME, mistakenly thinking he is there to serve them, adopts their theory. In murders between people who know each other, the police are usually right and no harm is done; but when they are wrong, lives are forfeit. Sometimes there is no murder, and a man is found guilty of a crime that didn't take place. This is what happened to Leonard Barco, a janitor for a toy store who was caught in the grindings of the system, unable to extricate himself.

On Sunday morning, April 28, 1985, Gail Morris, a thirty-year-old black woman, was found dead in the front seat of a rusted and abandoned red Volkswagen, together with a collection of beer cans and empty vodka bottles. She had lived in

Plainfield, New Jersey, and spent much of her time drinking with Leonard Barco, a forty-five-year-old black man who was married. Her blue snorkel jacket was lying across the roof of the car. Its presence led to her discovery.

To the police, Barco was the obvious suspect. He had been seen drinking with Morris the previous Thursday night. Her brother-in-law saw them Friday morning, and a friend saw them Friday night at a liquor store. No one else saw her alive after that.

On Sunday, the day Morris was found, the police took a six-page statement from him in which he confessed to fighting with Morris but not killing her. They had been together Saturday night, he said. She was drunk, he got more vodka, and they continued to drink together. She also took some pills. He stayed with her until about 11:00 P.M. and left after they fought about his going home to his wife. She picked up a broom handle that was lying on the ground and hit him with it. He hit her back.

On Monday, the ME of Union County, Dr. Gennaro Braga, who had held his job for over fifteen years, autopsied Morris. He saw marks on her neck and small bruises on her chest and back, but could not explain the cause of death. The police, who had already interviewed Barco, told Braga they thought he had killed her. Braga, who was not a pathologist, took their word for it, and even though Morris had no neck fracture, he decided she had been beaten and strangled. The death was now officially a murder.

Braga had interpreted his findings as being consistent with the suspicions of the police. As commonly happens, they told him what they wanted him to say, and he told them what they wanted to hear. But he disagreed with one thing. He didn't think Barco had gotten the time of death right. Barco had said that he had been with Morris on Saturday night and that she had been alive when he left her. Braga thought Morris had been dead for over twenty-four hours. This put the murder at about midnight of Friday the 26th.

On the strength of Braga's autopsy findings, the police arrested Barco and got a second confession from him. This one followed the line of Braga's interpretation. In it, Barco admitted to strangling Morris. He had been too upset to say so the first time they questioned him, he told Detective La Vigne—he got excited when a lot of people were around him—but he was telling them the whole truth now. He also became confused about the time he was supposed to have killed Morris. He switched from Wednesday to Thursday to Friday, but the police got him straightened out. Eventually, they convinced him he had killed Morris early Friday morning, not on Saturday night as he had originally said. He was remorseful. "I feel bad because I killed Gail," he said.

The police also thought they would have a stronger case if they could show that Barco had lied. In their report they noted that they found misstatements and discrepancies: in his first confession Barco said he struck Morris once; in his second, he struck her three or four times. To their way of thinking, they had caught him in a lie, which made him guiltier. Barco, unaware of the report, applauded the proceedings: he had been "treated like a man," he said; Detective La Vigne had been nice to him, but he did not like the other investigators.

The police had made every effort to fit the confession to the postmortem report, but a few facts didn't quite conform to it. The most glaring inconsistency was Morris's disappearance. She wasn't in the car during part of the time she was supposed to be dead. The car was parked near her sister's house, and her sister, Priscilla Diane Morris, saw it every day when she went out in the backyard to feed her Doberman pinscher. On Saturday, Priscilla's children were playing out back with a bat and ball, and the ball rolled under the car. Priscilla went under the car after it. As she later explained to the police, if Gail had been in the car, she would have seen her.

But if the case didn't all hang together, there was nobody else to pin the murder on. And it seemed reasonable for Barco to have done it. He languished in jail for eight months awaiting trial. At the end of that time, the public defender of New Jersey asked for my opinion about Morris's death. States that have capital punishment, as New Jersey does, also have legislative guidelines regarding its use. All murders are not equal. Someone has to decide whether the level of viciousness is enough to warrant the death penalty. In the past it was simpler—if the jury decided you were guilty, you were executed. Now there are nuances and calibrations. One way to measure the heinousness of the crime is by the pain and suffering of the victim. Was the victim conscious? For how long? The public defender wanted advice on whether the murder was heinous enough to sentence Barco to death.

When I looked at the evidence, I saw a number of discrepancies. Gail Morris had health problems that might have contributed to her death. She was a drug addict and an epileptic and had been hospitalized in the past for grand mal seizures. The hospital had given her medicine, but there was no evidence that she was taking it. Epileptic seizures can be triggered by alcohol, and if they are severe enough and last long enough they can cause death, but there would be no way to know whether that had actually happened. The bruises on her neck did not point to anything definite, either. They were just bruises, the kinds that are common to alcoholics, who often bump into things. Morris's windpipe was not fractured; there were no hemorrhages in her eyes. In fact, there was no evidence at all that she had been murdered. On the other hand, she had 0.46 percent alcohol in her blood, an amount high enough to cause death. She had probably overdosed on alcohol.

Other evidence put the time of death much later than Friday, and confirmed Barco's original story. The pictures of Morris showed unhatched maggot eggs in her eyes. Maggots have a reliable biological cycle. Their development from egg to worm to fly follows a predictable timetable. The stage and condition of those eggs was almost as good as having a clock. In my experience, flies deposit their eggs on people just after death or while they are unconscious. Between the time they are laid and the time they hatch, maggot eggs last less than twenty-four hours. Therefore, Morris must have been dead less than twenty-four hours when she was found on Sunday morning. If she had been killed on Friday, the eggs would already have hatched.

Rigor mortis also proceeds inexorably, and it told the same time as the maggot eggs. Rigor was extensive when Morris was found. It is at its stiffest twelve hours after death, and takes twelve hours to disappear. On Monday, when the body was autopsied, it was gone. Rigor could not have lasted from Friday night to Sunday morning.

Finally, there was the commonsense evidence of the blue jacket, the jacket that nobody stole. Morris's blue jacket was lying across the top of the car like a banner. In her ghetto neighborhood, a good blue jacket would not have lasted twenty-four hours—it would have vanished long before Sunday morning, when she was found. Morris was probably alive on Saturday and wearing her jacket.

Dr. Braga, who signed the autopsy report, did an extraordinary thing—he admitted to the judge that he had made a mistake. Few of us have the grace to apologize. He hadn't known about Morris's alcohol level. He had sent tissues to the lab, but he had not seen the results. Afterward, when the search continued for witnesses, people turned up who had seen Morris alive on Friday and Saturday. Barco was released from prison.

This story had a happy ending. The review system saved a man from the ultimate injustice. For the most part, it is the poor who get into this kind of trouble, but the cause—faulty forensic diagnosis—can be found on every level of society. Under different circumstances, Claus von Bulow, who had command of millions, had the same problem.

Claus von Bulow was accused of twice trying to murder his wife, Martha "Sunny" Crawford von Auersperg von Bulow, socialite and utilities heiress, with insulin injections. Between December 1979 and December 1980, Sunny was hospitalized three times in a coma. In the first episode at Newport Hospital, Dr. Janis Gailitis diagnosed her as having bronchopneumonia. He also noticed that she had low blood sugar. After she recovered, her New York doctor, Richard J. Stock, gave her a glucose tolerance test. Over a period of six hours, the test will show a high sugar level for diabetics and a low one for hypoglycemics. Sunny's sugar level went low. After four hours it was down to 23, and Stock diagnosed idiopathic hypoglycemia (low blood sugar of unknown origin, probably natural). The normal blood sugar level is considered to be between 80 and 120, but normal is what is normal for you. During exercise, a normal blood sugar of 100 can go down to the 20s with absolutely no ill effect. You don't get into serious trouble until it gets near zero. Sunny could manage very well at 23.

Early the following December when the von Bulows were in New York, Claus found his wife unconscious and rushed her to Lenox Hill Hospital. Her speech was slurred and she had a head injury, and Dr. Stock thought she might have a blood clot on her brain. But blood tests showed her pH to be very acid. Doctors pumped out her stomach, gave her fluids, and restored her electrolyte balance. Stock diagnosed "involuntary aspirin toxicity in the course of treating a severe headache." Sunny had overdosed on aspirin. She had taken at least sixty-five tablets, well above the lethal level for many people. Aspirin makes the blood acidic. The body's pH changes from alkaline to acid, preventing the enzymes from functioning properly. It is impossible to take sixty-five pills accidentally, without noticing it. Aspirin is not a cumulative drug. The pills all have to be taken within a short period of time.

The aspirin overdose was a failed suicide attempt. Nobody would say it, so Sunny wasn't offered counseling. Most of the successful suicides we see have already been seen by other doctors in the two or three months before their death. This was not just a cry for help like Robert McFarlane's, or a superficial wrist slashing. Most people would have died. There was no question of insulin.

The final hospitalization came three weeks later. On Sunday morning, December 21, Claus found Sunny unconscious on the marble floor of their bathroom at Clarendon Court, her Newport mansion. The window was open; it was 5 degrees Fahrenheit outside, and she was hypothermic—her temperature was down to 81 degrees when they got her to the hospital. It is rare to survive such a low temperature. The heart starts beating irregularly when the temperature falls to the mid-80s. Sunny was literally within minutes of death. Had von Bulow waited longer, she would have died. Judging from the way she was found and from the open medicine cabinet, the EMS people thought it was an alcohol and barbiturate overdose. The admitting doctors, who also considered her age and the fact that she had no history of illness, agreed. They took a blood sample and gave her a glucose test (this is one of the first things hospitals do when someone is brought in unconscious from unknown causes) and quickly learned that her blood sugar was 29. It was an abnormal finding, and they focused their entire attention on it. Usually, the hospital staff begins treating a suspected overdose right away, even before the lab results come back, but they were diverted by the glucose. Unaware that she functioned well with an even lower blood sugar level of 23, they thought that must be the cause of the coma. It was a misdiagnosis. Four hours later the lab phoned in the alcohol and barbiturate levels. The doctors discounted them. They were already working on the premise of low blood sugar.

They started her on an IV, which raised her glucose level. An hour or two later they drew a second blood sample, and the lab tested it for glucose. The glucose level was higher because of the sugar in the IV, but Sunny remained in a coma. The doctors asked the lab to test for insulin, but the lab technician didn't think it was necessary to test both samples and threw one out.

(Later, a great deal of confusion arose over which one of these samples was actually tested.) Insulin controls the glucose level in the body by "eating" sugar. If the sugar level is high, the pancreas produces more insulin to process it. If the sugar level is down at 29, where Sunny's was, the pancreas should stop producing insulin.

Sunny remained in a coma. The hospital lab sent the blood specimen to a more sophisticated lab in Boston, but something went wrong. The first time it got a 0.8 reading of insulin. The lab tested a second time, and the result was 350 units. (Ten to 20 units is normal.) Such a disparity usually indicates that something is drastically wrong with the specimen. The lab sent the sample to its main laboratory in Anaheim, California, to try a third time. A few weeks went by before the results came back. Anaheim got yet another number—216 units—and reported that number to the hospital. It seemed like a reasonable number. Intravenous glucose, such as Sunny was getting, can normally shoot the insulin level to over 216. No injection was necessary to arrive there. However, the high insulin level was used as evidence that Claus had injected Sunny. It was the scientific basis, the crux of the charge. An insulin level of 216 units is much too high to coexist with a blood sugar level of 29. It suggests insulin poisoning—unless the insulin and blood sugar are not coexisting at all, and the numbers come from two different specimens.

After being told that an excessive amount of insulin had put Sunny in a coma, the family became suspicious. Maria Schrallhammer, Sunny's fiercely loyal maid, who had been with her for twenty-eight years, remembered seeing insulin in a black bag. (Claus, who was very amusing, had been known to refer to her as "Mrs. Danvers," the housekeeper in *Rebecca*.) The black bag and its contents sat at the center of the case like some dark malevolent totem. It was of dubious provenance. Claus said it belonged to Sunny, but he thought that her son from her first marriage, Prince Alexander von Auersperg, had tampered with

it. Alexander said it belonged to Claus. Everyone denied owning
it. It was an orphan.

There were several sightings of it. Maria first saw the bag in
a closet in Sunny's Fifth Avenue apartment and then again at
Clarendon Court, on December 19, 1980, two days before her
mistress was found unconscious. The bag was filled with drugs
(including an exotic variety of Valium in the form of a yellow
paste, not available in the United States), syringes, and several
needles. Later, Maria saw a small glass vial of insulin. "Insulin,
for what?" she asked, taking her suspicions to Alexander. He
and his sister, Annie-Laurie, called Ala, hired Richard Kuh, a
lawyer and former New York City district attorney, to conduct
an investigation. They looked for the bag and found it a few
weeks later in January 1981, inside a locked closet at Clarendon
Court. There was no insulin in it. One of the needles had been
used.

In the course of preparing for the trial, the prosecution tested
the used needle and found that the outside of it was caked with
insulin. This was interpreted as proof that it had been injected
into Sunny, a conclusion that makes no sense at all. Needles
don't work that way. After an injection, there is no drug left
on the outside of the needle. The skin and tissues collapse over
it as it is withdrawn, and wipe it clean. Traces of the drug remain
in the inner bore of the needle, but not on the outside. In any
event, the black bag and everything in it was tainted, having
been handled by Claus's accusers before it got to the Rhode Island police.

Claus hired Herald Price Fahringer as his defense lawyer.
Fahringer was the quintessential defender, tall, handsome, and
silver-haired. His bearing was aristocratic, his tailoring impecca-
ble. He had recently handled one of the Jean Harris appeals. He
called me in to consult before the first trial.

When I looked over the records, I was struck by the amounts
of alcohol and barbiturates. The alcohol level in Sunny's blood
was 0.01 when she was brought to the hospital. This is low, but

if you consider the rate at which the body absorbs and breaks down alcohol, it indicates a very high level in her blood when she collapsed at home. She had not drunk any alcohol from the time she lost consciousness in the bathroom until the time the tests were taken—a period of eight hours. The body burns up about 0.015 gram per 100 cc of blood every hour. That is one shot of whiskey or one can of beer per hour. After eight hours, her body would have burned up .12 gram—that is, eight drinks—and there was still some left.

She also had the equivalent of ten to twelve capsules of amobarbital in her blood, which by itself is enough to cause a coma. That level would also have been higher at the time of her collapse. But the hospital doctors looked at Sunny's condition from the point of view of treating it. If it wasn't dangerous, it didn't have to be treated. They didn't think she had enough amobarbital in her blood at the time she was hospitalized to be in danger. They didn't count back eight hours. And they were misled by the low blood sugar.

The alcohol and barbiturate levels and the aspirin overdose added up to a typical suicide attempt, the same kind I saw all the time in my job, except for the mansion and the marble floors. It reminded me of Edwin Arlington Robinson's poem about Richard Corey: he was "richer than a king," the envy of all the townspeople, but they saw only the superficial glitter; they didn't know anything about him. "And Richard Corey, one calm summer night,/Went home and put a bullet through his head." Suicide made sense psychologically, too. People who fail at suicide don't just give up—they keep trying until they succeed (assuming they are serious about it). Sunny tried twice—once with aspirin and then, three weeks later, with alcohol and barbiturates.

If I was wrong, if Claus had tried to murder her, he did it with barbiturates, not insulin.

I told Fahringer there was no insulin, that Claus was being tried for a murder attempt that had never taken place, and Sunny was in an irreversible coma because the doctors had misdiagnosed her. He might have grounds for a malpractice suit against the hospital, and I thought such a suit could strengthen his hand in the courtroom. But Fahringer did not believe it was his job to develop a malpractice suit. It was his job to see that Claus was found not guilty. He didn't go along with my suicide theory, either. In his view, there was no evidence of it, and he couldn't just come out of left field and claim suicide. No one in Sunny's family had ever suggested such a thing. More likely, Sunny was abusing drugs and kept taking larger and larger amounts and drinking more and more until she went into a coma. Even so, the general belief in the insulin theory was over-powering. It had been accepted by virtually everyone on its face value. In order to counter it and prove suicide, Fahringer needed extrinsic conditions—proof that Sunny was depressed or had been telling people that she didn't want to go on living. Other-wise, his credibility with the jury would dwindle, and so would his effectiveness.

Rather than gamble Claus's freedom against such high odds, Fahringer chose a two-pronged defense: Claus was innocent and it wasn't insulin poisoning, but if it was, there were other ways of explaining it, such as Sunny's abuse of drugs.

At the trial, he focused on the blood-test mixups. Altogether, there were two blood samples, two tests for glucose (one on each sample), and three tests for insulin. The first glucose test was taken when Sunny was rushed to the hospital in hypothermia with a blood sugar of 29. When the doctors took the second blood sample, Sunny was already being treated, absorbing sugar water from the IV. Her sugar level would be high, and the insulin level would have risen to meet it. So a high insulin level in the second sample would mean nothing. One of these blood samples was sent to the lab to be tested for insulin. One of them was thrown out. Which was which? The rest of the mixup centered on the three different test results for insulin and the fact that the lab had arbitrarily chosen the one that came out at 216 units.

The three different results invalidated the entire exercise. There was no way to know how much insulin Sunny had in her blood.

Fahringer didn't think he needed to belabor the three different laboratory results. It was enough that the lab had tested the wrong specimen for insulin. He interviewed the two hospital technicians who had handled the samples. One of them told him she thought she had thrown out the first sample (taken before the IV) and she agreed to testify to it, but she changed her story on the witness stand. Under oath she swore she did everything right—it was the second sample that was thrown out and the first that was tested for insulin.

Other things fell apart, too, for their own perverse reasons. Fahringer had bad luck with his witnesses. Joy O'Neill, a woman who had worked in an exercise salon in Manhattan (since closed), testified that Sunny came in often. They developed a friendship, and Sunny told her how she injected herself with insulin to lose weight. This story might have created a stir, but the salon's records, which the prosecution dug out at great effort, showed that Sunny had rarely gone there. Did the witness lie? Were the records wrong? Fahringer thought that Sunny's appointments were off the books for tax purposes, but the testimony undermined his case.

Two of the doctors that Fahringer relied heavily on were not persuasive with the jury. Dr. Milton Hamolsky, of Brown University Medical School, was pressed by the prosecution into admitting that he could not rule out an insulin injection as the source of Sunny's coma. The second doctor, John Thomas Carr, chief psychiatrist at Newport Hospital, diagnosed her as "neurotic and desperately in need of psychotherapy," and testified that she could be classified as suicidal. But Carr hardly knew her. He had gone to her room to interview her after her first coma, and had reached this conclusion after an acquaintance-ship of about twenty minutes.

This ineffectual showing of the defense witnesses did not make much of a dent in the prosecution's case. Dr. Richard J. Stock,

Sunny's New York doctor who prescribed her sleeping pills and tranquilizers, testified against Claus. Stock had given Sunny the original glucose tolerance test and diagnosed idiopathic hypoglycemia. At the trial he said that Sunny's hypoglycemia was a nonserious disease, and she would not have gone into a coma from it. The coma had to be caused by an insulin injection. He had accepted the prosecution's numbers—the 29 glucose combined with the 216 insulin.

In addition to Stock, Stephen Famiglietti, the chief prosecuting attorney, lined up a team of Harvard Medical School professors to testify against Claus. They may have been brilliant at treating natural diseases, but they were out of their element when it came to diagnosing poisoning. They had no way of evaluating whether the lab tests made sense. None of them questioned the premise. They simply draped their opinion on the faulty structure of the insulin theory—that Sunny's low glucose and high insulin equaled poison.

Dr. Harris Funkenstein, a prominent Boston neurologist, testified that there could be only three possible causes for the coma—an insulin-producing tumor, a liver disorder arising from alcoholism, or exogenous insulin (injected from the outside). Having set up his own straw man, he then knocked it down: tests had established that neither of the first two causes applied; therefore it had to be the third. Funkenstein also thought the coma could have been "self-induced," as he delicately put it, but Fahringer stuck to his original plan and did not pursue this line of questioning. There had been no previous evidence of Sunny's injecting herself.

Dr. George Cahill, affiliated with Harvard Medical School and an expert on diabetes, also testified that injected insulin was the only possible explanation of Sunny's coma. Fahringer asked if he would still think the same thing if the insulin test was invalid, and Cahill replied that it didn't matter; it had to be insulin anyway because the sugar level was so low. Everyone lost sight of the fact that it was 23 during Stock's glucose test.

The doctors were equally uninformed about the levels of alcohol and barbiturates. Not having been trained in forensic pathology, they weren't suspicious enough and didn't have the background to ask the right questions; they didn't realize that the levels must have been very high when she went into a coma. Funkenstein dismissed the barbiturate level—it was too low to mean anything, he said. Cahill thought it was possible the barbiturates had contributed to the coma, but they couldn't have caused it—barbiturates have no effect on blood sugar. Therefore, it had to be insulin. None of the experts appreciated the significance of the earlier aspirin overdose.

By their testimony this clutch of prominent experts, unschooled in forensic medicine, gave weight and authority to a meaningless insulin test. They were presented with an assumption—that 29 glucose and 216 insulin meant that Sunny had been poisoned with an insulin injection—and they never questioned it. But Claus was very impressed with them. He identified with them socially. He sat there listening as one after another they put the noose around his neck and tightened it, and thought how admirable they were.

Later, during his appeal, I told him they were off the mark. "Oh, they were quite good," he said. "Yes," I said, "they were good but wrong." He looked puzzled. They were honorable men, didn't I understand? He regarded them as a connoisseur would, judging them on the basis of style, not substance. His sense of status completely dominated his code of values. Even though the doctors were wrong, he would be more likely to accept a false statement from a member of the club than the truth from an outsider. He had no animosity. I was not so dazzled. To me it looked like another case of the best and the brightest making a mess for everyone else to clean up.

I also thought that some of the main characters in the drama had something to protect, and might not be entirely unhappy if Claus were found guilty. Dr. Stock would be absolved of any problem that might arise from prescribing barbiturates. The hospital would be out from under a misdiagnosis and possible malpractice suit. The Harvard experts need never be questioned about the quality of their expertise. Sunny's children would avoid the stigma of having a mother who had tried suicide, and they wouldn't have to share her money with Claus. None of these matters was of overriding importance, but still, a guilty verdict would be convenient.

For its own reasons, the jury thought so, too. In March 1982, Claus was found guilty on two counts of attempted murder, based on Sunny's first and third hospitalizations. The aspirin overdose fell through the cracks.

Shortly after his conviction, Claus hired two new lawyers, Alan Dershowitz and Thomas Puccio. Dershowitz was in charge of finding grounds on which to appeal the verdict, which he did; after he won the appeal, Puccio handled the second trial. Like Fahringer, both lawyers were prominent if not flamboyant. They courted cameras and reporters and publicity. Dershowitz appeared frequently on Ted Koppel's *Nightline*. Puccio had just triumphed in the Abscam convictions, which sent a U.S. senator, among others, to jail for accepting a bribe.

Dershowitz gathered evidence to persuade the court that the first trial was legally defective and raised questions about the old evidence. Fahringer had laid the groundwork for an appeal by objecting in all the right places during the trial. He also helped to publicize Truman Capote's recollections of Sunny, which were used in the appeal.

Capote went on talk shows and gossiped about his friendship with Sunny. She drank a lot, he said, and she took drugs. He knew for a fact that she had injected herself with insulin in order to lose weight. This was not exactly new—Joy O'Neill, the woman in the exercise salon, had said the same thing—but O'Neill's evidence had been discounted, and her presence on the talk-show circuit would never have had the same fascination as Capote's did. Dershowitz understood that judges read the newspapers and are influenced by human as well as legal arguments.

While Dershowitz and Puccio were figuring out strategies, Claus called me. He had seen my name in Fahringer's records and wanted to talk about the medical and scientific evidence. I first met him at a working dinner in Sunny's fourteen-room Fifth Avenue apartment. Sunny was lying in a coma in the Harkness Pavilion at the Columbia-Presbyterian Medical Center. Two of Dershowitz's law students were working out of the apartment. Money was tight. The bulk of Sunny's $75 million estate was all tied up, and there was a strong possibility that Claus would never see the $14 million he was due to inherit on her death. The will didn't say anything about a coma. Meanwhile, he was living on the interest from a $2 million trust—$120,000 a year—and feeling squeezed.

Claus, always a gracious host, greeted me at the door wearing a smoking jacket. He mentioned that his daughter, Cosima, had attended the same school as mine, and joked about our notoriety: between us, we were keeping the *New York Post* in headlines, I with my fight with Koch and he with his attempted murder. The apartment was palatial, with marble floors, antique furniture, gilt mirrors, and a library full of leather-bound books that had an unopened look about them. Andrea Reynolds, Claus's Hungarian-born companion, was there, along with her third husband, Sheldon Reynolds, the television producer. Sheldon apparently had not yet read in the gossip columns that his wife was having an affair with Claus. Andrea, who had strong opinions, had taken it upon herself to coordinate the defense. She had a great deal of common sense and was very protective of Claus. His first batch of lawyers had let him down, she said, and she was anxious to develop the medical and scientific evidence. Claus was afraid it would get lost in the legal technicalities of the appeal.

Dinner was a tunafish casserole.

We had several dinner meetings, and I told Claus about my suicide theory at one of them. Even though he had everything to gain from it, he rejected the idea. "I don't think she would commit suicide," he said. He seemed to feel it would be worse for people to think that he had driven his wife to suicide than that he had killed her.

My role in the appeal was to evaluate the accuracy of the insulin levels which Fahringer had shied away from. Dershowitz and Puccio were high on it and had no qualms about trampling on Claus's delicate feelings. My affidavit had three themes: first, that insulin was not involved at all in Sunny's first episode in December 1979—her doctor in Providence, Janis Gailitis, had diagnosed bronchopneumonia; second, that Sunny was suicidal, and the aspirin overdose (the second episode) had to be a suicide attempt; finally, that Sunny had continued her suicide threat in the third episode, an alcohol and barbiturate overdose.

Dershowitz had a deadline for the appeal, and I worked to finish my affidavit on time. So did my associates, Dr. Robert Shaler, the serologist, and Dr. Leo DalCortivo, the toxicologist. After all the urgency, Dershowitz's assistants were in no hurry to pick up the documents. They were going to collect Capote's deposition first. I was a little miffed about this. I thought the gossip was trivial, and it disturbed me that Dershowitz was treating our work like second-class material. But it didn't matter. The judges overturned the verdict on a legal technicality, and the state decided to retry Claus.

At the second trial, which was televised, Puccio asked me to sit at the table with him when the prosecution experts testified. He wanted me to interpret medical and scientific evidence and tell him which questions to ask. Some doctors do this. I am uncomfortable doing it because it gives the jury the impression that I am an advocate, not impartial. I did agree to watch the trial on television at home, after which we would discuss his questions for the next day.

Puccio called me from Providence one Sunday, worried about an unsettling development. The prosecution claimed to have uncovered new evidence. Dr. Jeremy R. Worthington, a neurologist who had gone to Oxford and was on the consulting staff at

Newport Hospital, was being billed as a star witness against Claus. Worthington had seen bruises and scratches on Sunny at the hospital, the kinds of marks that looked as if they had been inflicted by another person. The prosecution had an inflammatory theory to match the bruises—that Claus had held Sunny down and injected her with insulin. He had first tried to knock her out with a barbiturate injection so he could inject the insulin more easily. Sunny tried to prevent him and they struggled, hence the bruises.

The theory was absurd. It was superfluous for Sunny to have two reasons to be unconscious. Why inject two drugs when one will do? The theory made more sense applied to a suicide than to a murder attempt. Suicides often use more than one drug, just to be sure. But Puccio was worried. The idea put a whole new sinister slant on their relationship, and Claus, who had been convicted once, was sinister enough already. He asked me to look over the hospital records to see if the theory had any merit and, if not, to see if it could be destroyed. He didn't want Worthington to testify.

There were several peculiar things about the theory. First, the bruises and scratches. It was not at all strange for Sunny to have marks on her body. Worthington had seen her the day after she had been admitted to the hospital. During those twenty-four hours, the hospital people would have tried to save her life; their efforts could easily have left bruises. They usually do. Just the act of lifting her onto the stretcher from the bathroom floor where she was found could have left bruises. But why was Worthington, a neurologist, talking about bruises and scratches? A neurologist knows about nerves. It was not within his professional competence to interpret Sunny's bruises as signs of a struggle—much less to take the leap and say that she was being held down and injected with insulin. He was being allowed to testify in an area outside of his expertise because court rules do not draw such narrow distinctions. The rules say that an M.D.

can testify on anything medical, whether he is board-certified in that area or not.

I also wondered why Worthington hadn't come forward before. Where had he been during the first trial? Surely the evidence of the bruises had been there then, too. I asked Puccio how the prosecutor had found him. It turned out that Worthington had found the prosecutor. He had volunteered his services. This was disturbing news. In my experience, witnesses who volunteer have to be doubly scrutinized because of possible conflicts of interest and yearnings for the limelight.

Even beyond these considerations, there was something strange about the whole thing. Why was this man, a neurologist, going to testify when the real expert on insulin was nowhere in sight? Where was the chief ME of Rhode Island, Bill Sturner, who knew about bruises and who had published papers on insulin poisoning and hypoglycemia? In the normal course of events, the prosecution would have called Sturner as a prize witness. Could it be that he had not been helpful to them? That he had not been able to corroborate the prosecutor's theory of insulin poisoning?

Worthington's curriculum vitae was a little unusual, too. On the witness stand he had testified that he had gone to college at St. Edward's School in Oxford and to medical school at the University of Bologna. The University of Bologna has a long, proud history. Its medical school, one of the oldest in Europe, was very prestigious during the Renaissance, but since then it had declined precipitously. Academically speaking, it wasn't in the same league as Oxford. Why had Worthington gone to such an undistinguished medical school where classes were conducted in Italian?

We called Claus. Claus knew everyone. He and Andrea Reynolds, whose marriage had by now disintegrated, had a room across the hall from ours at the Biltmore Plaza Hotel. Claus sauntered over, wearing an elegant gray silk robe. Claus knew Worthington. He also had a good friend who lived in Oxford and offered to call him. In addition, one of the legal assistants, Andrew Citron, called his brother Zachary who was studying history at Oxford, and offered him $50 to find out if Worthington had actually gone there. It was 9:00 A.M. in England, Monday morning, but we still had the rest of the night before having to appear in court. Zachary called the university records office. The school had no record of Worthington. Oxford University didn't even have a college named St. Edward's.

Later that morning, in a hearing with the judge (no jury) on Worthington's qualifications, he was asked again about his college, and this time he modified his original answer. St. Edward's, he explained, was an English public school in the town of Oxford. It had no connection with the university. He had not gone to college at all. Instead, he had lived in Italy for a few years, and then enrolled in the University of Bologna's medical school. Although he had taken two forensic medical courses there, the judge decided he was not qualified to discuss the origins of Sunny's scratches and bruises, and he was not allowed to testify. Bill Sturner, the ME who had been notably absent at the first trial, didn't testify in this one, either. Not having seen Sunny in the hospital and having no knowledge of her history, he was unwilling to say that her bruises were the result of a struggle.

Puccio relied on my affidavit and suggestions and argued to the jury's satisfaction that insulin poisoning was not the cause of Sunny's coma but that alcohol and barbiturates were, and that it could have been a suicide attempt. The black bag, which was a dramatic physical thing, lost its position as a centerpiece, and its influence waned. The jury brought back a verdict of not guilty and Claus walked out free, but the case had by this time moved into another realm, beyond a simple yes or no. Claus's world is still divided into people who think he was unjustly accused and people who think he got away with murder. It probably always will be.

12

ATTICA

WHO DID IT?

ALL THROUGH THE summer of 1971, unrest was building in Attica, a maximum security prison in upstate New York, and by September the prisoners had a pile of unresolved grievances. When the riot came, it was triggered by a small incident—a prisoner threw a can of food at a guard, and his privileges were taken away. The next day, Thursday, September 9, the riot erupted spontaneously in Cell Block A after breakfast. Prisoners from all four cellblocks (A–D) surged down the corridors toward "Times Square," the crossroads of Attica, where a guard stood at his post. The guard, William Quinn, slammed down the gates, but one of them had a faulty bolt, and the prisoners broke through. They beat Quinn and left him lying in a coma with a fractured skull. They took forty hostages.

The state police were called in. Led by Captain Hank Williams, a hulking three-hundred-pounder, they began retaking the cell blocks, fighting their way through with tear gas and guns. Before they could retake the fourth (D), and against Williams's advice, they were ordered to stop. The prison authorities were getting more and more worried about the hostages, and they lost their nerve. The decision was a mistake. In prison riots, the longer you wait, the more chance there is that someone will get killed. There are always enmities in prison. During a riot, when the prisoners are no longer protected by guards, people try to get even.

Russell G. Oswald, the commissioner of corrections, began negotiations. The prisoners set up committees and asked for help from outsiders they trusted. Tom Wicker, the *New York Times* columnist and author, was one; Louis Farrakhan, who later became the leader of the Nation of Islam, was another. The negotiators met with the prisoners in D yard, where there was also a complement of reporters and television cameras. The prisoners had twenty-eight demands, including better food and medical care. Oswald agreed to all but three of them. He refused to remove Vincent Mancusi as superintendent of Attica, he refused to grant total amnesty, and he refused to allow passage to a Third World country to those who wanted to go.

About fifteen prisoners were running the insurrection, led by Roger "Champ" Champen, Frank "Big Black" Smith, and Herbert X. Blyden. Most of the others in the cell block were supporting it. If they weren't, they at least knew enough not to say so—except for two of them. Barry Schwartz and his friend Kenneth Hess talked to one of the reporters covering the story, and Schwartz slipped him a note saying that not all the prisoners were in favor of the uprising. The reporter brought the note to the leaders, who accused Schwartz and Hess of betrayal. They were taken away and their throats were slashed—but not fatally. Schwartz was later seen leaning out the window with a towel around his neck, yelling for help. It was a brief reprieve. The other prisoners pulled him back in, and the leaders decided that he and Hess had to be killed. The next day the prisoners took Schwartz to an empty cell and laid him on a mattress on the floor. A circle of inmates handed around a knife and each of them stabbed him many times. They did the same to Hess in a different cell. It was a group effort; it made each inmate equally guilty of murder, and they were bound to silence in mutual defense. A third man, Michael Privitiera, was killed the same way. He was erratic and violent and was inciting fights among the prisoners. All three of the dead prisoners were white ethnics— two Jews and an Italian—outside the mainstream of prison culture, which was predominantly black ghetto.

On Saturday the 11th, William Quinn, the guard at the crossroads, died in the hospital. So there were four deaths, three of them not known to those outside the walls, before Attica was retaken.

By Sunday, the third day of negotiations, Oswald was increasingly frustrated by the lack of progress. Amnesty was the sticking point. The prisoners knew Quinn was dead, and they were insisting on a pardon. Oswald and Governor Nelson Rockefeller were more and more worried that the prisoners would kill the hostages. They were threatening to slash their throats. All of the observers could see that the prisoners were armed with knives and spears from the tool shed. Samuel Melville, a 1960s radical who was known as the Mad Bomber, was in there, and he was probably stockpiling Molotov cocktails. The prisoners had dug trenches in D Yard—it looked like the Western Front in World War I. The guards also thought the prisoners had guns.

On the morning of Monday the 13th, the prisoners turned down Oswald's final offer. Within minutes the troopers went in. They had wanted to go in all along, and Rockefeller finally agreed. It had lasted four days.

Rockefeller issued orders that none of the corrections officers were to join in the retaking of the prison. They were too emotionally involved. They had been humiliated by the uprising; they were angry at Quinn's death, and they wanted to save their fellow guards who were hostages. They would be looking for revenge. Some of them went in with the troopers anyway. Later, they said they hadn't heard the order. One of the hostages was shot in the chest and killed with a bullet from a handgun that belonged to a corrections officer.

Just before the troopers went in, a helicopter flew over the yard and dropped tear gas. The prisoners took eight hostages up to the catwalk overlooking D Yard, blindfolded them, and stood behind them, holding knives to their throats. They thought this would prevent any forcible retaking of the yard, but the troopers brought in sharpshooters, each aiming at a single prisoner on the catwalk. Other troopers charged into the yard, firing shotguns. The shotguns contained double-O buckshot, which has 9 or 12 pellets per cartridge. It is commonly used for riot control. The troopers fired rapidly for a few minutes. Then it was quiet. The prisoners surrendered.

Thirty-nine people died in the retaking of Attica. Thirteen were hostages. The rest were prisoners. Hank Williams, who led the state troopers, was unfairly made the scapegoat. He wasn't promoted for years.

The prisoners didn't have guns or Molotov cocktails after all. They did have knives and sharp instruments, and some of the hostages were cut. Early eyewitness accounts coming out of the prison confirmed what everyone expected—that the hostages were killed by the prisoners. The dead hostages were brought out wearing bloody blindfolds around their necks. The press and the assembled throng believed that the prisoners had behaved true to form and carried out their earlier threats.

No single mortuary was large enough to handle all the bodies, and they were sent to a number of different places in the Rochester and Buffalo area. The majority of them—nineteen inmates and eight hostages—went to Rochester, and the first medical news (as distinct from the eyewitness news) came from there. John Edland, the ME of Rochester, reported that everyone had died of bullet wounds. Most of the hostages had head wounds from double-O buckshot. That was how their blindfolds got bloody. None of the hostages had a slit throat. On Tuesday, Edland's story was in the newspapers. It was extremely unpopular with the guards.

Edland's analysis came as a terrible shock to Oswald and Mancusi, the superintendent. It was plainly beyond belief, and Oswald decided to get a second opinion. I was recommended to him, and I flew to Attica. The prison rose from the plains like a huge medieval fortress, with turrets and thirty-foot-high walls. The stench of tear gas emanated from it.

When I walked in, Oswald and Mancusi stared at me in dismay. They had expected someone older, more buttoned-down, someone more bureaucratic, like Dr. James Bradley, the official who had recommended me. I was thirty-seven, had long hair, and looked like a hippie. Bradley reassured them that I was not a wild man. Oswald, who was pained and concerned about the deaths, wanted the bodies of all thirteen hostages reexamined. He was certain there had been a mistake. He and Mancusi thought the hostages had been beaten and abused for days, and he had seen with his own eyes that the hostages' throats were cut. They had been up on the catwalk with knives at their throats and the troopers had gone in to save them. And now Edland was saying that the troopers had killed them. It made no sense. Oswald's first reaction to me was that there was a communist plot of some kind. Why else would Edland lie? He and Mancusi didn't want me to bother reautopsying the prisoners; they just wanted me to do the hostages.

The idea that Edland would be part of a communist plot did not seem plausible to me. He was known among MEs as a right-winger. He was also very good. I said I had to look at *all* the bodies, prisoners and hostages, and that to understand one death, I had to understand all of them. To do it properly, I had to reconstruct the scene, see where the bullets came from and where everyone was standing, find patterns of injury. I was not there to prove that Edland was a liar. If I couldn't examine all the bodies, I said, I would rather not do any. I would return to the city.

My response gave them an out. Mancusi, who had an us-against-them attitude, became very irritated with me. He didn't want it done that way, and he was quite ready to dispense with my services. Oswald thought about it, however, and decided I made sense. He said yes.

I stayed from Wednesday to the following Monday. I looked at the hostages first. Most of them were in funeral parlors, embalmed and ready for burial. The death certificates had been written. Some of those who had been on the catwalk had cut marks on the back of the neck and one had a stab wound in the stomach, but none of these injuries had caused death. Edland was right. They had all died of bullet wounds, and the shots had come from a distance. There was no powder or soot on the skin. One prisoner, who was in a tunnel in the yard, died of a shotgun blast to the left thigh—he bled to death. Judging from the three-inch spread of the double-O shot, the nearest weapon had been nine feet away. (Shotgun pellets spread about one inch per yard.) Six of the hostages had died of a single shot to the head, which looked odd, like an execution, but could be explained by their positions in the yard. One of the troopers had discharged his buckshot at a prisoner who was making a threatening gesture, and missed. From where he was standing, the pellets would wind up 150 feet away, spread out at head height. A group of hostages was standing in a circle blindfolded in just that spot.

By Tuesday afternoon, a controversy was raging over Edland's analysis. Was he deliberately misleading everyone? One of the funeral directors called a press conference. He could prove that Edland was lying, he said. The body he had prepared for burial had been beaten to death by a prisoner, and Edland had falsely said it was shot by the troopers. There was no bullet wound in the body. The troopers were being given a bum rap.

The funeral director also subscribed to the conspiracy theory. He thought there was a cover-up, that somehow "they" were trying to appease the prisoners. The community in general agreed that there was a plot to blame the deaths on the troopers rather than on the prisoners. The corrections people lived near the prison, and the community supported them.

I looked at the body of the guard who supposedly had died of a beating. His eyes were indeed blackened, and he had other bruises. I turned the body over. There was a gunshot wound in his back. The funeral director hadn't seen it. While he was preparing the body he had tipped it this way and that, but he had never turned it over completely. The guard looked as if he had been beaten, but the coloration of his bruises was faded. It had probably happened on the first day of the riot. In any event, he hadn't died of his bruises; he had died of the bullet wound. It was late at night when I found the bullet hole, and the funeral director was out. I telephoned him to come and look. He rushed over carrying his bowling ball. Then he went to the phone and called his wife. Honey, he said, don't say anything else to the newspaper reporters.

After doing the guards, I reautopsied the prisoners. They had not been identified. Each had a number. In his hurry, Edland had left some of the bullets in them. There was a question about one of them, Elliot Barkley. Arthur Eve, a black state assemblyman from Buffalo, who was one of the outside negotiators, claimed that Barkley, a leader of the uprising, had been deliberately killed by the troopers as punishment. During the four days, Barkley had been very vocal, criticizing the system on television. Some of the prisoners said they saw him alive after the retaking, but Edland's autopsy report said he died of a single rifle shot in the back. Eve and others interpreted this as an execution. When I reautopsied Barkley, I saw the single rifle shot, but it was a very big hole—too big for the bullet. The bullet had gone in sideways. It was a tumbling bullet (like the one that hit John Connally in Dallas); it had hit something else first, which meant it hadn't been meant for Barkley originally. When the prisoners realized that the execution couldn't have happened, they waffled about having seen him alive.

Within a few days after the surrender, there were charges of brutal retaliation, of prisoners being made to run a gauntlet of guards, of punishment and injury. The State Investigation Commission impaneled a grand jury, which came down with forty-two indictments against sixty-two prisoners, listing over twelve hundred charges, most of them centered around the taking of hostages. One prisoner, John Hill, was tried and convicted for killing Quinn, the guard. Over forty other trials were planned, but civil rights groups protested that all the indictments were against prisoners and none against the guards—the guards should have been indicted for their post-riot vengeance. Governor Hugh Carey, who was elected after Rockefeller's term, set up a commission to look into the charges of unfairness. The commission agreed that it was "selective prosecution," and on New Year's Eve, 1976, Carey decided to "close the book" on Attica. He pardoned seven inmates and commuted the sentence of John Hill.

Part of the fallout from Attica was the establishment in 1974 of a medical review board to monitor the deaths of prisoners. I've been a member since the beginning, and we have been able to change some conditions. Many prisoners were dying of what local doctors said were heart attacks. The guards had told the doctors so. (There are no prison pathologists. Bodies are handled by the local coroner. In the past, he did not autopsy most of them.) Investigating these deaths, we found the telltale signs of a choke hold—pinpoint hemorrhages in the eyes and bruises on the neck. Now, all prison deaths must be autopsied.

Other deaths were caused by the effects of tear gas. When prisoners became unruly, guards would put on masks, throw canisters of tear gas into their cells, and then, still wearing masks, go in and beat the prisoners. Inmates were dying from lung irritation and pneumonia. We succeeded in having a law passed forbidding guards to use tear gas unless it had first been approved by the superintendent. Since that time, there have been no deaths from tear gas.

Suicides were the principal preventable cause of death. Most of the suicides had given warning; they had threatened to kill themselves before they actually did it. We made the guards aware that the threats should be taken seriously and that counseling should be provided. With the knowledge that they are accountable, that someone is watching, the prison authorities have a different attitude. Medical care is better. We've cut down on the number of suicides and on all unnatural deaths.

Something positive came out of Attica: the kind of public service medicine that is a natural outgrowth of our profession. MEs all over the country should be similarly engaged, but such a policy is more the exception than the rule. The system has been failing for some time, undermined by the dearth of untrained MEs and the politics of death—the primacy of political over medical considerations. We should be trying to attract more medical students to forensic science. We should raise the salaries and status of MEs and banish their fears of being fired for meritorious service. We should encourage states to improve the quality of forensic science services and make them available to all on request. We are not doing any of these things.

These reforms are important, but by themselves they are not enough to turn the system around. Before anything can be done, there must be a change of attitude—a recognition that a problem exists and an appreciation of the value of forensic pathology.

INDEX

Academy of Forensic Sciences, 4
Adams, John, 35
Adam's apple, 38
Addison's disease, 14
adrenal cortex, 14
age, determination of, 37–38, 86
Albano, Edwin, 160, 161
alcohol, 2, 37, 39, 73, 190, 195–96
  in von Bulow case, 193, 195–96,
    199, 203
algor mortis, 39, 90, 92–93
amobarbital, 196
amyl nitrite, 181
anatomy, asymmetry of, 37
Andre, Carl, 75–76
Ann Arbor, Mich., veterans
    hospital in, 42–43
Antistius, 24
apnea monitor, 113–14
Armed Forces Institute of
    Pathology, 7, 9–10
Arnold, William J., 162–63
Aronson, Marvin, 142, 149
arsenic, 40, 41–42, 44
arson, 172
arteries, coronary, 36, 37–38
aspirin, 192, 196
Attica prison, 207–15
autoerotic death, 178–80
autopsies, 36–39
  incisions for, 36
  Judaism and, 97–100
  natural vs. unnatural death and,
    3
  past restrictions on, 49

public opinion of, 50
time required for, 36
toxicology tests included in,
    39

Bailey, F. Lee, 154
Balabin, Pinhas, 95, 96, 97
barbiturates, 2, 39, 46
  in von Bulow case, 193–204
Barco, Leonard, 187–91
Barkley, Elliot, 213
Baselt, Randall, 178
Belushi, John, 90–95, 141
benzoylecgonine, 177–78
Bhopal chemical disaster, 41
Billings, Richard N., 20
Blackbourne, Brian, 74
Blakey, Robert G., 19–21
blood sugar level, in von Bulow
    case, 192–206
Blyden, Herbert X., 208
bodies:
  decomposition of, 100–101
  determining age of, 37–38, 86
  disposing of, 46
  identification of, 77, 78–82,
    84–86, 88–89
  jurisdiction of, 88, 89
body snatchers, 50–51
bones, identification of, 81, 85
Bradley, James, 211
Braga, Gennaro, 188–89, 191
brain, 38, 93
Branson, Frank, 174
Brawley, Tawana, xi–xii

217

About the Authors

DR. MICHAEL BADEN received his medical degree from New York University in 1959. He worked as a medical examiner for New York City for twenty-five years, and was chief Medical Examiner from 1978–1979. He is currently executive director of the Forensic Sciences Consultant Unit of the New York State Police. He teaches at a number of medical and law schools, also writing and lecturing extensively about forensic medicine. He lives in New York City with his family.

JUDITH ADLER HENNESSEE is a writer whose feature articles, profiles and reviews have been published in THE NEW YORK TIMES, ESQUIRE, VANITY FAIR, and many other magazines. She won the 1986 Front Page Award for distinguished journalism for her media column in MANHATTAN, Inc. She lives in New York City.

DATE DUE			